Seeking God First

SEEKING GOD FIRST

A Practical Plan for Finding Joy and Peace in Him

BY ANITA KEAGY
with Bethany McShurley

Seeking God First: A Practical Plan for Finding Joy and Peace in Him

Copyright 2023 © by JoyShop Ministries. All rights reserved.

ISBN: 978-1-7353792-3-4 (paperback)
978-1-7353792-5-8 (hardback)
978-1-7353792-4-1 (ebook)

All Scripture quotations, unless otherwise indicated, are taken from the Holy Bible, New International Version® NIV® Copyright © 1973, 1978, 1984, 2011 by Biblica, Inc.® Used by permission of Zondervan. All rights reserved.

Scripture quotations marked NKJV are taken from the New King James Version®. Copyright © 1982 by Thomas Nelson. Used by permission. All rights reserved.

Scripture quotations marked AMP are taken from the Amplified Bible, Copyright © 1954, 1958, 1962, 1964, 1965, 1987 by The Lockman Foundation. Used by permission.

Scripture quotations marked NLT are taken from the *Holy Bible*, New Living Translation, copyright © 1996, 2004, 2015 by Tyndale House Publishers, Inc., Carol Stream, IL, 60188. All rights reserved.

No part of this publication may be reproduced, stored in a retrieval system, or transmitted in any form or by any means—electronic, mechanical, photocopy, recording, or any other—except for brief quotations in printed reviews, without the prior permission of the author.

Photo by: Carrie King
Cover design: George Pytlik
Editing & formatting:
www.ChristianEditingandDesign.com

To the Shepherd and Overseer of my soul, who saw this wounded and straying lamb and gently led me back home.

*"But seek first his kingdom and his righteousness,
and all these things will be given to you as well."*
– Matthew 6:33

CONTENTS

Acknowledgments — xi

Introduction — 1

PART 1: UNDERSTANDING KEY PRINCIPLES OF SEEKING GOD — 9

CHAPTER 1 The Blessing of a Repentant Heart — 11

CHAPTER 2 The Wisdom of Opening God's "File" Often — 27

CHAPTER 3 The Exercise Our Souls Need: Prayer — 39

PART 2: PRACTICAL SUGGESTIONS FOR SEEKING FAITHFULLY — 57

CHAPTER 4 Start Each Day the Right Way — 59

CHAPTER 5 Remember the Rewards of Relationship-Building — 81

CHAPTER 6 Beware of Common Enemy Tactics — 103

CHAPTER 7 Keep Pursuing God Himself — 123

CHAPTER 8 Take the 21-Day Challenge — 137

Leader's Guide — 155

Appendix: How to Know You Are God's Child — 179

ACKNOWLEDGMENTS

AS I PREPARE to release this book, I know I can't do so without expressing thanks for some of the many wonderful people who have supported me throughout its development. First, I am grateful for my wonderful husband, Paul; he has always believed in my call to ministry and has supported me every step of the way. Our children, Shelly, Carrie, Josh, and Ryan, have also encouraged my passion and cheered me on to the point of securing me invitations to speak at their school's chapel. I don't think I would be where I am with the Lord without my family's steady support.

Gratitude also extends to the thousands of people who, over the years, have either written me a personal note, sent in financial support, or upheld JoyShop Ministries—my workshop-based outreach that teaches others how to seek God for themselves—in prayer. These faithful brothers and sisters in the Lord have kept my feet moving forward when I felt overwhelmed and had brief moments of doubt.

I also feel thankful for those businesses and ministries that have supported JoyShop. The Pocket Testament League, for instance, partnered with us to give JoyShop our own Gospel of John cover, "Letter from God." Soteria Productions, based in Atlanta, Georgia, worked hard to professionally produce my original Bible study series, "The Joy of Seeking God First," from which this volume was developed. Vision Video discovered that series and gave us a much larger audience than I ever dreamed of.[1]

Finally, I'm also deeply appreciative of my board of directors. Their wisdom and guidance have protected me over the years, from both myself and my impulsive nature.

I see every one of those listed—and my dear writing partner, Bethany McShurley, too—as a blessing from God, a teammate in the work He has called me to do. For them, and for the message He has put on my heart, I praise Him.

---

[1] Please note that while this video content is available online and for purchase, it is not a necessary supplement to this study or the related group experience and differs from this volume chronologically.

INTRODUCTION

"We are apt to pay more attention to our newspapers than to God's Book."[1]
– Oswald Chambers

HAD SOMEONE TOLD me twenty years ago that truly seeking God for myself every day rather than just listening to weekly sermons and reading occasional devotional thoughts in between them could bring me joy and peace, I would've been mildly intrigued. After all, I had certainly experienced a measure of that when following Him closely back in my college days—and who doesn't want such things? Still, I would've only smiled politely before mentally dismissing the idea. *Who has time for that in midlife?* I might've thought. *Pastors? Nuns? Those who want to become little old Sunday school teachers? Certainly not me.*

I was a church-going mother who had four kids still living at home; they seemed to need me at all hours. Some days I felt like I was racing uphill on the ever-moving treadmill of life. Every day I grew just a little more frustrated and exhausted by all the worries that come with raising a family, running a busy household, keeping the weeds out of our landscaping, and trying to keep my marriage on track. And as the months passed, I found myself starting to get a little whiny about how "rough" my life was becoming. "Why is

---
[1] Oswald Chambers, *The Highest Good with the Pilgrim's Song Book and Thy Great Redemption* (Grand Rapids: Discovery House, 2015), n.p. Kindle.

it that no one in this family seems to care or want to help me?" I'd fuss under my breath.

It was in this same season that I started to allow magazine covers and TV commercials to have more sway in my mind. I let them convince me I was a closet failure, not just in how I was running our home but also in terms of my looks. "Be thin!" they shouted at me. "Exercise! Buff up! Don't you know it's every American woman's job to look like a model?" I was deeply aware that the only way that was going to happen was if I shipped my kids off to boarding school and made my appearance and body shape the focus of my life. Still, obsession with my imperfections nagged.

Moreover, I started to grow irritated with some of the messages I was hearing at church—not because I disagreed with them, but because somewhere along the way I'd started believing it was entirely up to me, and not the Holy Spirit within me, to live them out. For instance, I knew I was supposed to produce fruit matching my identity as a Christian: love, joy, peace, patience, kindness, gentleness, and self-control were to be things people associated with me (see Galatians 5:22–23). But every time I tried to get through even *one* morning of displaying them all together, my kids would press my buttons so hard I wanted to run away.

Yes, twenty-five years into my marriage, pressures were mounting on every side as I continually tried and failed to achieve the impossible: I wanted to be a perfect wife and a perfect mother with the perfect body! And while it would've been nice were I able to be the perfect Christian too, that goal seemed even less attainable. Worries over what impact my combined failures might have on my marriage, my children's futures, my desire to serve the Lord, and the way God thought about me consumed my thoughts. Though I labored hard, I knew I was only spinning in circles. And frankly, my faith was starting to suffer.

Earlier, in the 1980s, there'd been a commercial for Wendy's restaurants. In it, a pair of elderly ladies expressed disdain for hamburgers that didn't have as much meat as they did condiments. "Where's the beef?" they would ask before the announcer assured viewers that Wendy's burgers would not fail them in this department: a Wendy's burger has plenty of protein. One day as I returned home from running errands during the worst of the struggles I've described, the ladies' stated frustration in that commercial rose to the top of my thoughts. "Where's the beef?" Somehow it just seemed to get to the heart of all my troubles.

On that particular day, my negative thinking had reached a peak. I felt haunted by the notion that my life was totally failing to deliver the kind of joy that seemed to come so easily to my godly parents and dedicated church leaders like my pastor. I lacked peace and any sense of true purposefulness or contentment. Years before, I'd memorized John 10:10, where Jesus said, "I have come that they may have life, and have it to the full." But the hamburger of my life, when it came right down to it, was much more about pushing through on self-effort and putting on a good face than it was about delivering the kind of fullness He surely meant. And deep down, I was miserably tired of that.

When I pulled into the garage that afternoon, I opened the car door, stepped out, and asked aloud, "So, God, where's the life?"

And with that question ringing off the garage walls, I stomped into my living room, hung up my keys, and looked up at the ceiling. (Keep in mind I was the only one home.)

"I am one of Your children," I whined to the Lord. "You've been a part of my life for a long time. You've seen me through so much! You know I believe the words You spoke in John 3:16: 'For God so loved the world that he gave his one and only Son, that whoever believes in him shall not perish but have eternal life.' So, I know without a doubt that I'll spend eternity with You, but I'm sure not living the 'full' life here!" (Actually, it went through my mind to add that I was like a hamster spinning round and round on a silly wire wheel about to come off its axis, but I figured He didn't need to hear that.)

Looking back, I'm not sure why God chose to answer me that day. But I suspect He'd been waiting a long time for me to start crying out to Him with a heart that was at least softening toward the idea of being reshaped. Whatever the reason, while I did not hear an audible voice, the gist of one particular Bible passage came to mind. I couldn't remember the whole, but I knew that in it Jesus Himself addressed chronic worriers like me. And years of attending Sunday school had given me a good idea of where to find it.

I reached for my Bible and turned to Matthew 6. Here's what I read:

> "[D]o not worry about your life. . . . Look at the birds of the air; they do not sow or reap or store away in barns, and yet your heavenly Father feeds them. Are you not much more valuable than they? Can any one of you by worrying add a single hour to your life?
>
> "And why do you worry about clothes? See how the flowers of the field grow. They do not labor or spin. Yet I tell you that not even Solomon in all his splendor was dressed like one of these. If that is how God clothes the grass of the field, which is here today and tomorrow is thrown into the fire, will he not much more clothe you—you of little faith?
>
> ". . . *But seek first his kingdom and his righteousness, and all these things will be given to you as well.*" (Matthew 6:25–30, 33, emphasis mine)

For the first time in my life, verse 33—rather than the parts about the birds and flowers—stood out to me. That five-letter word *first* in the last sentence practically jumped off the page! Suddenly I could see that I'd been spending the vast majority of my time obsessing about my life, my schedule, my marriage, my kids, my shape, my worries. And aside from keeping the most basic commitments in terms of church life, I knew I'd long neglected to really seek God or what He wants at all. I'd rationalized my way right out of anything close! Yet the Bible was telling me to seek such things *first*. Could it be that prioritizing Him was the very thing I needed?

In the next minutes God slowly opened my mind to accept that I'd been living as a so-called follower of Jesus Christ for decades. Even though I'd grown up singing songs like "Seek ye first the kingdom of God, and His righteousness,"[2] and was forever proclaiming things like "Jesus is Lord of my life," and though I'd seen for myself how much God loved me and how generously He provided for me, I had *failed* to make our relationship a priority. Though God had shown me nothing but steadfast love and grace throughout the course of that relationship, I'd only been deceiving myself into thinking I was a faithful follower.

> Might prioritizing God be the very thing we need?

In that sacred hour of awareness, I felt compelled to pull out my dictionary. When I looked up the word *first*, I found this: "earliest in time or order, of topmost importance."[3]

At that, I actually winced. In no way had I been making the pursuit of God a matter of "topmost" anything.

Then I heard the Father speak to my heart, not audibly, but much as the conscience does: "Anita, herein lies your problem. Every day when you wake up, you make that day all about you and everything you feel you have to accomplish. Yes, you do have a lot of responsibility with rearing four children and helping with the

---

[2] Karen Lafferty, "Seek Ye First," with The Maranatha! Singers, track B3 on *The Praise Album*, Maranatha! Music, 1974, vinyl.

[3] Eugene Ehrlich, Stuart Berg Flexner, et al., *The Oxford American Dictionary: Major New Edition*, s.v. "first" (Oxford, UK: Oxford University Press, 1998), 217.

produce business. But for years you have prioritized these things over spending time with Me. And where has it gotten you?"

I knew the answer to that. It had led to the very frazzled, dissatisfied existence I'd been complaining about.

"You don't have the full life I promised My followers because you aren't tending to our relationship first," the Lord said. "You've tried putting *your* kingdom first for most of your life, and you know it doesn't bring fullness of life or the peace and joy you crave. Give Me a chance! Spend time with Me every morning before your busy day begins. Then just you wait and see what happens."

I'm deeply embarrassed to admit I didn't immediately agree to take Him up on this offer. I stubbornly hardened my heart and actually told Him I was just too busy!

You see, I knew without being told that He was urging me to spend time reading Scripture. To actually slow down long enough to sit and pray and reflect as a matter of course. Yet I didn't think the idea at all maintainable. After all, years prior I had tried to have morning devotions on a consistent basis. But getting sidetracked and allowing other priorities to take over had been hallmarks of that effort. Occasionally, when I'd heard a good sermon or message on the radio during that season, I'd felt inspired to try with diligence again—only to fail again. Wouldn't it be better not to try than to risk giving God that kind of half-hearted, yo-yo effort at relationship building once more?

Nothing in me really changed that night. In fact, the next morning, I got out of bed and began my daily routine as usual. First on the agenda was making my morning coffee. As it was brewing, I headed out the door and down our driveway to retrieve the newspaper. That was always my step two. But as I marched to the house at my usual hurried pace, God might as well have hit me over the head with the paper I'd been so eager to get because His voice at work on my heart stopped me cold.

"Anita," He said, "right here is where you go wrong. You start every day by grabbing the news and reading it for twenty minutes while you sip coffee. By the time you're done, you usually feel depressed and overwhelmed by all the problems and evil in the world. And with that outlook, you go to wake up your kids and start their day. You told Me just yesterday that you don't have time to spend with Me. *That's a lie.* Instead of starting with the paper and its bad news, why not begin your day reading My good news for those same twenty minutes?"

Thoroughly humbled by that, I returned to the kitchen for my mug of coffee and headed to my living room, where I kept my Bible in a basket beside an upholstered chair. I sat down, opened the book, apologized to God, and asked Him to show me what I should read and to help me understand it.

A remarkable thing happened then! Whereas for years my "times with God" had been little more than a matter of my reading an out-of-context Bible verse or two based on whatever devotional thoughts I'd picked up at the local bookstore, followed by my hurrying back to regular business, that day I began to consider God's Word differently, to read it more slowly, more thoughtfully, to really start considering how to "order my life" around it as my pastor always encouraged our congregation to do. And as I did, I began to sense its value not just as a time-honored religious text that can give a little general guidance now and then but also as a resource written directly to my heart from God. By the time twenty minutes were up, I actually felt I knew Him a little better, felt motivated to send up a little prayer not just for His help but also to say a sincere thanks, and was ready to wake my children with a lighter heart.

Just that easily, things began to change for the better in my home. That glorious morning, in fact, God started to change *me*: I slowly became a persistent God-seeker. And though life continued to have its stresses and there are even now plenty of times when I feel cultural pressures telling me I don't measure up, I came to prioritize my relationship with Him first. No matter what. And I can testify that it is one of the best decisions I ever made.

Today one of my favorite quotes by Oswald Chambers is "Five minutes with God and His Word is worth more than all the rest of the day."[4] I have come to understand the truth of this statement, and rarely will I miss my time with my wonderful heavenly Father. My time with Him sets me off on the right foot; it helps clear my mind of the world's noise. And it positions my heart to live, think, and respond God's way.

Since I began seeking God first, joy and peace have stopped being things I long for but are blessings I now experience. No matter what's going on in my life or the world. Closeness with God is no longer something I assume is reserved for Bible heroes and Bible scholars. And that frantic, fussy feeling I once knew all too well? It visits my heart far less often.

My prayer is that through regularly repenting, engaging with God's Word, and spending time in focused prayer at the start of your own days, you too will soon come to know the precious sense of closeness and other blessings that come with seeking God first. May the Holy Spirit use my experiences and the insights I share in the pages ahead to get you—and perhaps a group of friends—started on that journey.[5]

If you've trusted in Christ as Savior and are ready to get serious about beginning each day with Him, the joy and peace you desire really are within reach.

---

[4] Oswald Chambers, *The Oswald Chambers Daily Devotional Bible: 365 Daily Readings from the Author of* My Utmost for His Highest (Nashville: Thomas Nelson, 1993), 1028.

[5] A Leader's Guide for facilitating a small group based on this content is included in the back of this book.

PART 1:

Understanding Key Principles of Seeking God

CHAPTER 1

THE BLESSING OF A REPENTANT HEART

*"These people honor me with their lips,
but their hearts are far from me."*
– MATTHEW 15:8

LOOKING BACK ON my early years, I've come to understand that I was very fortunate to be raised by parents who loved and honored God with all their hearts and strived to raise us five kids with the same sense of duty. Because of their personal faith commitment, by the time I was five years old, I had a basic understanding of the truth that God created me and loved me and that I am unique and special to Him. I could retell all kinds of Bible stories—especially those about how God sent Jesus, His Son, into the world to die and come to life again so He could save those who'd trust in Him. Young as I was, I knew that salvation meant God's forgiveness of personal sins as well as the promise of Heaven. And one Sunday night while I was listening to a men's quartet at church, I began feeling conviction in my heart that I needed Jesus's help for myself. It grew so strong that I went home afterward and cried and told my parents I wanted to invite Jesus into my heart. They knelt with me by my bed as I did.

It was on that long-ago night that I began my journey as a

Christ-follower and claimed my identity as a child of God (see John 1:12). Naturally I was too young and naïve to understand that this did not mean that I would live a perfect, sinless life—that is, never miss the mark for how God wanted me to live. Moreover, at that point I had no idea that my life could become one of honoring Him with only my lips and not my life. It would be years before I'd look back and see how much my life would reflect those of the ancient Israelites of the Old Testament, who waffled back and forth in living in obedience to God throughout their history. But most likely you can relate to my personal experience. Even if you've rightly called yourself a Christian for years, there's a good chance you haven't always lived in light of what Jesus did for you, what God says about you, or what He wants for you either.[1]

That common tendency is why discussion of seeking God must begin with a look at the topic of repentance.

I really meant it when I trusted in Jesus as a child. And throughout my girlhood, I went through the motions of attending church multiple times a week, praying regularly, and living by what I was taught the Bible said. Yet about the time I started facing the temptations common to the teen years, a definite gap between who I am as a daughter of God through Christ and how I was living began to appear.

My godly parents have always been wonderful gifts to me and my siblings. I can honestly say I never heard them talk in a mean tone to each other or say unkind things about other people. They never raised their voices. (Well, there was that one time when Dad yelled, "Good lands!" over something exasperating.) Yet when I was a teenager, I decided privately that my parents were out of touch with the modern culture I was living in and they couldn't

---

[1] If you feel any uncertainty about whether God sees you as His beloved child, or if you haven't trusted in Christ as Savior, please pause to read the brief article "How to Know You Are God's Child" at the back of this book before continuing this chapter.

relate to my world. In fact, I was just sure I knew better than they did.

On no point did I disagree with them more strongly than on the topic of boy-girl relationships. Mom and Dad had all kinds of restrictive rules about dating. In fact, I clearly remember how our family was sitting around our dinner table one evening when my mother made the announcement that none of us kids were to kiss anyone until we were engaged. (She felt that was reasonable since she and Dad had abstained from kissing until their wedding day.) They also didn't want us going to dances or the movies. In fact, those particular pastimes were absolute no-no's for many rural pastors' kids like me back then—not because dancing and movie watching are unbiblical but because of concern that immoral things might come of them. Since I felt those rules were foolish and unrealistic, I smiled politely at Mom's words and continued to sneak behind their backs to do as I wanted.

By the spring of 1974, my senior year of high school, my parents had accepted an invitation to move our family to Lancaster, Pennsylvania, so they could pastor a larger congregation in our denomination and be nearer to relatives. We were scheduled to relocate that June, right after prom. I didn't mind the upheaval since I had plans to attend Messiah College (now Messiah University) in Grantham, Pennsylvania, soon after. Far more concerning was the knowledge that my parents would probably forbid me from going to prom since it involved dancing, and there was no way I was going to miss the biggest event of my senior year! Thus began the process of trying to convince them to let me attend.

For weeks I wore my poor mother out on the topic. I literally begged her and Dad to allow me to go. Finally, reluctantly, they agreed that I could attend with my latest boyfriend, who was sixteen, a junior in high school. Known for his strong Christian values, he was a church-going guy and a real goodie-two-shoes! That won them over, along with the fact that he respectfully accepted their terms that we not stay for the dancing.

Leading up to the big night, I made plans with a friend so I could dress at her house and then sleep over there afterward so my parents wouldn't know how late I'd stayed out. When the highly anticipated moment came and my boyfriend and I arrived at the big event, I took in the whole "Over the Rainbow" theme with a sense of deep pleasure that I'd gotten my way. It was all I'd anticipated it would be! Still, once the dancing started, I stayed true to my word and obediently left the party with my date. After a little aimless driving around town, however, we parked the car in a dark and secluded spot.

We never meant to go as far as we went that night. For a while, we just sat there and talked. Then talking led to kissing. And kissing led to ... well, you can guess. Frankly, everything happened so fast that our consciences barely had time to kick in. But when they did, we immediately stopped our sexual exploration and drove back to my friend's house in awkward silence.

By the next morning, I felt terrible about what had happened. I was a Christian, but I knew my actions had not evidenced that. Although I reminded myself we had not crossed the line of full penetration, I knew I still needed to repent and ask the Lord's forgiveness. It turned out that my boyfriend felt exactly the same way about what he'd done. So we got back together that day for the sole purpose of praying together and seeking God's forgiveness. Our physical closeness was never repeated.

The following weeks were busy for me as my family packed for our twelve-hour drive and move to Pennsylvania. Once there, we settled into an old farmhouse and began getting acquainted with the wonderful people at our new church. They were so welcoming and our new situation felt so exciting that it didn't take us long to adjust.

The only anxiety-producing problem I was experiencing in

this new setting involved my own strange health. I noticed my body was changing, and I couldn't fathom why. Since I was scheduled to begin college in a little less than a month, my parents decided to make me an appointment with a local doctor. The plan was to swing by his office on our way to a community picnic being held to formally welcome our family to our new church and town.

It was in that doctor's office, as I lay on the table in the examining room, that I heard these devastating words: "Young lady, you're pregnant."

Just like that, my life fell apart. Never in a million years did I think this could happen to me after one casual and careless sexual encounter!

As I headed out to the car beside my mom, who had been present for the doctor's announcement, I couldn't look at her. Even worse was when we got into the station wagon and I had to tell my father the shocking and devastating news! Silence and disappointment hung heavily in the air as we each processed how this would impact our family. In fact, I'm not sure we said anything at all even when we picked up my siblings to take them to the picnic event with us.

When we arrived at the park, the other kids in my family scattered as the three of us who knew my secret pasted on our happy-pastor's-family smiles and tried to carry on as if a bomb had not just been launched into our lives. After all, it seemed the only thing we could do. Yet it wasn't long before I slipped away from the pavilion, found our car, climbed inside, and began to weep.

In no time my father, having noticed I was missing from the festivities, came looking for me. I'll never forget the moment he opened the station wagon's door and slid into its middle seat beside me. Wordlessly, he put his arms around me and comforted me while I cried. While he easily could've scolded and shamed me or demanded, "How could you have done this to us, Anita? We're new at this church! This doesn't look good—the pastor's daughter being pregnant," he never condemned me. And Mom never would either, for which I am eternally grateful! In their wisdom and discernment they could sense that my own condemnation was working overtime, and they wanted me to repent on my own and find healing, not remain stuck in self-blame.

When we got home that evening, Dad said the three of us needed to get on our knees and ask God for His help. He didn't say what it was we needed God's help with: I knew. We needed wisdom regarding what to do about the baby inside me, what to do about my parents' first grandchild.

When we finished praying, Dad looked at Mom, then at me, and said, "Anita, you have a decision to make. You got yourself into this spot, and we cannot tell you what to do about it. Talk to God about this and see what He would have you do. We'll support whatever that is."

The diary entry I wrote in my room right after that shows just how hopeless and lost I felt:

> *"It's over. I'm pregnant. I don't understand why, but I am. Mom and Dad are broke up. No words to express how I feel. Sick. How will my life turn out? I love mom and dad."*

As I lay in my bed that night, I went not to the Lord but to a mental review of my options. After all, I knew I hadn't been living by His Word lately and didn't think He should have to bail me out of the mess I'd made. I realized I could (option 1) press my ex-boyfriend to marry me, although I wasn't in love with him; (option 2) choose to raise the child as a single parent; (option 3) place him or her up for adoption; or (option 4) get an abortion—which had become legal just the year before. Every one of those choices, I realized, would lead to a set of consequences that would impact me for the rest of my life. And the more I thought on it, abortion seemed the easiest and most convenient solution to my problem! After all, it was the one most likely to keep our relatives and the people at church from finding out about the pastor's "wild" daughter, and it just might spare me the embarrassment of my brother and sisters hearing about what had happened too. It also seemed to make the most sense given my plan to go to college and find and marry the man of my dreams.

By sunup, I'd convinced myself that having an abortion was the least costly way out of my mess. In retrospect, I can now see that Satan was out to destroy my child's life and mine by using the fear tactic. Fear had such a hold on me that I nervously went to my parents and said I was seriously considering having an abortion "just to save face!"

I'll never forget the way Mom and Dad looked long at each other and then back at me before Mom gently said, without an ounce of judgment in her voice, "Anita, that just isn't one of your options. We can't let you go that route."

The love shining through their eyes slowly drove out the overwhelming terror I felt, and I realized with a start how important it was that I stop thinking about my reputation or even theirs. I needed to give some serious thought to the life inside me.[2] So at their prompting I went to my bedroom and finally chose to have a long, personal talk with God.

As I closed my door, a familiar Bible verse came to mind. In Matthew 6:6 Jesus said, "Go into your closet and pray to your Father in secret" (my paraphrase). Frankly, the thought of hiding in a closet sounded comforting, so I walked directly into mine, sat down on the floor, wrapped my arms around my knees, and started to cry again. These sobs were not related to guilt or self-pity or frustration over the situation in which I found myself. They were tears of humble repentance; they evidenced my running to

---

[2] If you or someone you love has had an abortion, please visit https://hopeafterabortion.com/ or purchase a copy of Pat Layton's wonderful workbook *Surrendering the Secret: Healing the Heartbreak of Abortion* for support and encouragement.

my heavenly Father out of true brokenness over my choice to sin against Him, as well as my new sense of desperate dependence on Him. As they fell, I asked God to forgive me for all of my rebellion, including my selfish consideration of discarding the life of my little one, and to give me wisdom about what to do. Though part of me still felt that I didn't deserve His help so why ask, I clung to the knowledge that He was my only hope—not to mention my baby's.

In that sacred time of surrender, God's presence was so palpable. His peace settled over my body like a warm blanket. It was then, deep within my spirit, that I suddenly knew what He wanted me to do. As Moses's mother had entrusted her son into the care of Pharaoh's daughter (see Exodus 2:1–10), I was to place my baby for adoption and trust God to oversee the child's future. I was also to stop offering my parents surface obedience and start living with true respect to His Word.

To my family's credit, every member of my household chose to support me in this decision and to stick by me in the remaining six months leading up to the very difficult thing I'd agreed to do. My youngest sister, Lorene, even reminded me that as a Christ-follower—for that is what I was—I could hold onto the promise of Romans 8:28: "We know that all things work together for good to those who love God" (NKJV). Although that verse was a bit comforting, my honest thought—although I didn't want to disappoint Lorene in my response—was, "Yeah, right! How could God ever make good come from this?"

The larger my middle grew and the more active the baby became, the more deeply I fell in love with my child. At every precious kick, in fact, a feeling of nausea over our coming separation would wash over my heart. Nevertheless, about two months before my anticipated delivery date, I obediently set in motion what the Lord had prompted and then wrote this in my diary:

> *"I feel sick about giving my baby away. I went to the adoption agency today even though my heart said no. I met with them. They asked me what kind of home I wanted my child to be placed in. I was very specific in saying I wanted my child to be raised by a mom and dad who loved the Lord their God with all their heart."*

The request I'd made regarding who I wanted to raise my baby was a sign of my reignited faith as well as a kind of emotional life ring keeping me afloat. I reasoned that if my child could just be brought up hearing and benefiting from the good news about Jesus as I had, he or she would accept Him too. And that, I knew, would guarantee me the joy of spending eternity with my son or daughter.

Regardless, the week before I was to deliver, I continued to struggle with my decision. Had I heard God right? If so, how would I ever have the courage to go through with things? I must've said under my breath five hundred times, "God, I *cannot* go through with this!"

But on one such occasion, when I was in the car and the radio was blaring in the background, what the on-air preacher was saying pierced my heart. "Never doubt in the dark," he insisted, "what God told you in the light."[3]

Right after that, the Lord spoke to my anxious, grieving soul: "Anita, when you were in the closet that day, crying out to Me for help, you were in the light of My presence. You were allowing truth from My Word to ring in your mind, to help you think clearly. It was then that I told you what is best for you and your child. Right now you are letting your emotions make you feel that everything is dark, hopeless. *Hang on to what I told you in the light!*"

Again, I repented and pressed closer to Him.

---

[3] This quote has been attributed to minister and author V. Raymond Edman.

The morning of January 25, 1975, arrived; with it came the first birth pains. My parents solemnly drove me to Lancaster General Hospital, where my mother was able to attend me through the labor process as my dad paced the expectant fathers' area. At 3:18 p.m., after a long labor, I was told I'd given birth to a little girl. The nurse announced that she was seven pounds and thirteen ounces. As directed, I kept my eyes closed and didn't ask to hold the precious miracle whose cries squeezed my heart. Instead, I clung to the fact that I was doing what God desired and obeyed the adoption agency's now-antiquated advice to avoid making any contact with the one I'd carried for nine months. "Please, Jesus," I silently begged, "*help* me."

A couple of days later, after signing the final adoption papers in which I gave up all parental rights, I had to leave the hospital with empty arms. It was time to try to go on with my life. While I felt about as low as any human can feel, I took comfort in the knowledge I'd not have to face the future alone. God Himself would walk alongside me through the years ahead. I'd been reading His Word, and from it I knew that to be the case.

> The journey of seeking God begins with faith. But also key to it is repentance, allowing a deep sense of "I've not been honoring God and am truly sorry" to lead us to ask for His help to change.

Back in that teenage season when I claimed, "I'm a Christian," but basically just lived for myself, seeking fulfillment from this world and my interests, I conceived deep sorrow for myself and my family. Yet God not only gave me the privilege of bringing a tiny person into the world anyway, He also immediately and lovingly accepted my sincere repentance and began working in me to get me back on track spiritually and to guide me in walking in the light of His truth.

Of course, the journey of really seeking God begins with faith:

"Anyone who comes to him must believe that he exists" (Hebrews 11:6). But also key to it is repentance, allowing a deep sense of "I've not been honoring God and am truly sorry" to lead us to cry out for mercy and to ask for His help to change. After all, God Himself said, "I will return again to My place till they acknowledge their offense" (Hosea 5:15 NKJV). As surely as Israel had to admit, "We have sinned!" before receiving His help in defeating their oppressors, this is the only route to living in the blessings He has for those who seek Him (see Judges 10:15–16).

WE TEND TO think of repenting as something that those who haven't accepted Christ as Lord must do. And indeed they must. But it was to the church that John the apostle said, "If we confess our sins, [God] is faithful and just and will forgive us our sins and purify us from all unrighteousness" (1 John 1:9). Consider, for example, the case of Israel's godly King David, who allowed his lust for one of his married subjects, Bathsheba, to lure him into an affair and the murder of her husband. The Lord was so angry with David for choosing to sin against Him that He sent the prophet Nathan to tell him so (see 2 Samuel 11–12). But thankfully, by the time he sat down to write Psalm 51, David was ready to own what he'd done as the sin that it was and to repent because he knew it takes asking God's forgiveness to get back on track and move forward. He said,

> Have mercy on me, O God,
>   according to your unfailing love;
> according to your great compassion
>   blot out my transgressions.
> Wash away all my iniquity
>   and cleanse me from my sin.
> For I know my transgressions,

> and my sin is always before me.
> Against you, you only, have I sinned
>   and done what is evil in your sight....
>
> Cleanse me with hyssop, and I will be clean;
>   wash me, and I will be whiter than snow.
> Let me hear joy and gladness;
>   let the bones you have crushed rejoice.
> Hide your face from my sins
>   and blot out all my iniquity.
> Create in me a pure heart, O God,
>   and renew a steadfast spirit within me.
> Do not cast me from your presence
>   or take your Holy Spirit from me.
> Restore to me the joy of your salvation
>   and grant me a willing spirit, to sustain me....
>
> You do not delight in sacrifice, or I would bring it;
>   you do not take pleasure in burnt offerings.
> My sacrifice, O God, is a broken spirit;
>   a broken and contrite heart
> you, God, will not despise. (Psalm 51:1–4, 7–12, 16–17)

After penning this, David went on not only to enjoy restored fellowship with the Lord and to rely on His help through trials but to write even more psalms that speak to his renewed habit of seeking Him (see Psalm 63:1). He also went on to prepare his son Solomon to seek God and His wisdom for himself (see Proverbs 4).

If you opened this book on seeking the Lord in "I'm ready to get rolling!" mode, praise God! You may be walking before Him with a clear conscience already. But if you sense that things like a bad attitude, apathy, or willful sin are standing between you and

Him, please remember what God told you in the light, what you knew to be true when you first chose to trust in Jesus as your Savior.

The Lord Himself is your Rescuer. Your Redeemer. Your Righteousness (see Philippians 3:8–9; 2 Corinthians 5:21). He is the One who made you perfect at salvation and wants you to live in light of that (see Matthew 5:48). He is your Good Shepherd, the One who not only gave up His life for you but also offers you abundant life (see John 10:11, 14).

And you, simply because you trusted in Christ, are seen by God the Creator as His beloved child, as a co heir with Jesus (see Romans 8:17; 1 John 3:1)! You are treated not as your sins deserve or repaid for your failure to measure up to His standards (see Psalm 103:10–11). Rather, He has removed your sins as far as the east is from the west (see Psalm 103:12) and counts you among His saints (see 1 Corinthians 1:2).

It's God's desire that you know Him as a loving and good Father as well as a friend, that you enjoy awareness of His presence and peace on a daily basis—no matter what storms life brings your way. So determine today that you will not be robbed of intimacy with your Savior anymore. Then humbly repent of whatever wrong you've been indulging, asking Him to help you get back to doing life His way. That will open the door for the Holy Spirit to sweep into your days in a fresh way so that He can help you mature in your relationship with the Lord and find the joy and peace you crave. God said in 2 Chronicles 7:14, "If my people, who are called by my name, will humble themselves and pray and ... turn from their wicked ways, then I will hear from heaven, and I will forgive ... and ... heal." I can testify that God is faithful to do just that—and oh-so-much more.

Will you please spend the next few moments in prayer, asking God to "create in [you] a pure heart" poised to seek Him and to "restore to [you] the joy of your salvation" (Psalm 51:10, 12)?

TOPICAL REFLECTIONS

1. Second Chronicles 12:14 says, "[King Rehoboam] did evil because he had not set his heart on seeking the Lord." How did Anita find this principle to be true in her own life? How have you found it to be true in yours?

2. Read Psalm 66:18–20. What warning do you see in verse 18?

3. Read 1 John 1:6–10. What comfort do you find in verse 9 specifically?

4. What is something God told you in the light of His presence that you tend to forget when hard or dark times come?

5. Explain what humble repentance has to do with seeking God.

CHAPTER 2

THE WISDOM OF OPENING GOD'S "FILE" OFTEN

"Devote your heart and soul to seeking the Lord your God."
– 1 Chronicles 22:19

AFTER THAT BITTERSWEET day when my newborn daughter was given to her new parents, I stayed at home with my own family for the initial season of healing before going on to college as planned. Soon after that, I met my fun-loving husband-to-be, Paul Keagy. He accepted me and my past and had a knack for making me laugh when I was taking myself way too seriously. With the passing of time, we married and God blessed us with four beautiful children: Shelly, Carrie, Joshua, and Ryan. Yet as the years flew by, I never forgot my first daughter. Even though I had never seen or held her, I always quietly wondered in my heart where she was and how she was doing. On every January 25, her birthday, I would think about her and pray desperately that she was trusting in Jesus and sensed how much I loved her.

By the time I expected my first daughter to have entered high school, I felt certain she had been told she was adopted. But oh, how I hoped her awareness of me would translate into a curiosity about me—and perhaps even a determination to seek for me with the hopes of getting to know me! That, in fact, was my greatest wish.

One day it occurred to me that I should call the agency to update my records so it would always be easy for my daughter to find me if she wanted. When I contacted them, I discovered I had the option of starting a file for her. In it, I could put letters, pictures, and cards so that when she turned eighteen and legal ownership of the records would be accessible to her should she inquire, she could find that her birth mother had been stockpiling outpourings of affection for her for years. I was so excited to have a way to communicate how much I loved and missed her. Over the next few years, I began writing her letters. In every single letter I shared a little more about myself and my family and let her know how much I loved her and hoped to have a relationship with her if she desired.

"Oh, God," I prayed as I sealed each envelope I sent, "please help her want to find me and ask for the file!"

My first child's eighteenth birthday came and went without a word from the agency to suggest she'd requested her records. For the next three years, in fact, I received no notice that she had looked into her file at all. Each year that went by, my heart grieved a little more. Not only did I have to bear the sadness of not being able to meet my daughter, but I also didn't even have the comfort of knowing she would at least know who I was and how very much I loved her.

Finally, with Paul's full support, I decided to call the agency and ask if there was any way they could locate my daughter and tell her there was a file waiting for her. I insisted to the case worker I spoke with that I had no expectations and hadn't forgotten I'd given up all parental rights. "All I want," I said, "is for her to know she is loved and that I am open to a relationship with her if she likes."

For a fee and the filling out of several forms, the agency agreed to try to find her. They made no promises beyond that. Within a week, though, I received a call saying they had located my daughter. For the first time ever, I heard her name: Twila.

Just hearing her name brought tears to my eyes!

It turned out that twenty-one-year-old Twila had been raised in a local conservative Mennonite home and was now married to a young man, Daniel, with a similar upbringing. Not only was she married, but she'd also just given birth to a daughter, Emily, seven days earlier. Now I was a grandmother! Understandably, Twila was not ready to take meeting her birth mother on in the same season as adjusting to life as a new mom. She wasn't even ready to request her file. However, after discussing the situation with her husband and family, they all agreed the appropriate response would be to send me a polite letter through the agency to let me know how she was doing. When it arrived in my mailbox, I felt I'd been given the most valuable letter ever penned! When I opened it to see her handwriting and to read her thoughts, to see evidence that the baby who had grown in my womb decades before had grown into a woman, my heart pounded with excitement and joy. My eyes kept tearing up as my heart overflowed with thanksgiving to the Lord for this treasured letter I was now holding in my hands!

I immediately sent a handwritten letter back to her through the agency to thank her. And only a few weeks later, I received word she had asked for her file. (It would turn out that Twila was an avid reader.) Not long after she scanned through it for the first time—I still praise God for this—we began correspondence through letters exchanged via the agency. Oh, what a joy it was to get to know her through those letters she sent! And by reading the previous letters I'd placed in her file along with my new notes, Twila soon felt I was far less a stranger.

Finally, on July 16, 1996, my daughter and I met face-to-face. That was a *wonderful* day, better than I'd ever imagined! To see her face and to hold her in my arms for the very first time was a small taste of heaven on earth!

Praise God, today I not only have the joy of having Twila in my life—I also have the privilege of hearing her six children call me "Grandma." The Lord has been so good to me! My daughter and I have become friends, and I get to see for myself that she is living for Jesus—just as I'd long prayed. She even made a framed needlepoint for my wall that reminds me of that wonderful truth and her compassionate acceptance of me and our unconventional history. On it is Psalm 18:30: "As for God, His way is perfect."

Shortly after I met Twila and her family, I was having my morning quiet time with Jesus and reading through Acts 17. As typical then, my mind began to wander as I relived that magical day and moment of seeing my daughter's face for the first time. Joy filled my heart as I pictured the precious delight of holding her in my arms. Overwhelmed with gratitude but realizing that I needed to get back to the task at hand, I began to reread Acts 17. In it the apostle Paul is visiting Athens, a city that zealously worshiped the many gods and goddesses we associate with Greek mythology. Among the shrines to these many false deities, he finds a stone marker that says, "To the Unknown God." Never one to miss the chance to use a good illustration, Paul points to it and essentially tells the citizens that the one God they know very little about but are worshiping all the same is the God who created them and wants to be known. He goes on to proclaim,

> The God who made the world and everything in it is the Lord of heaven and earth and does not live in temples built by human hands. And he is not served by human hands, as if he needed anything. Rather, he himself gives everyone life and breath and everything else. From one man he made all the nations, that they should inhabit the whole earth; and he marked out their appointed

times in history and the boundaries of their lands. God did this so that they would seek him and perhaps reach out for him and find him, though he is not far from any one of us. "For in him we live and move and have our being." As some of your own poets have said, "We are his offspring" (Acts 17:24–28).

It was the word *offspring* that first jumped off the page and grabbed my attention! In that moment the Holy Spirit began a spiritual download that would forever change the trajectory of my faith journey with God and the way I look at the Bible. He reminded me that I was indeed God's offspring in the same way that Twila was my offspring. And just like my heart's desire was for Twila to seek and look for me so that we could enjoy an intimate relationship, so too His heart yearns for all His children to seek and look for Him, and He's not that far away! As I pondered this, the Holy Spirit brought something else to my attention. You see, I could never force Twila to want to look for me, and neither will God force us to seek Him! There had to be a desire within Twila's heart to want to know me, and so too with us! If there is no desire within a person's heart to know God, finding Him becomes an impossibility.

ONCE TWILA HAD the desire to seek me and learn about me, then she asked for the file at the agency and she began to read all the letters I had written to her. She quickly discovered how much I loved her and desired to be in a relationship with her, which opened the door to a more intimate friendship with her. God's Holy Bible is His File full of letters of love for us, expressing who He really is and what He really wants of us! Everything we need to know about Him is right there. So, why had I long neglected to regularly read and meditate on His Word? It was because I did not treasure His letters like I treasured Twila's. Over the years, I had slowly taken the Bible for granted, not realizing what a gift it is to have access to His written words! You see, every handwritten letter I received from Twila, I read slowly, trying to capture who she was because I wanted to know her intimately! Every letter brought me closer to her even though I had never seen her, and I read out of desire, not obligation. And I understood what a privilege it was to hold a letter from her in my hands! King David wrote in Psalm 119:11, "Your word I have treasured and stored in my heart" (AMP). *My Utmost for His Highest* author Oswald Chambers lovingly said of his Bible, "I hold in my hands the Thought of God."[1]

BEFORE TWILA STARTED reading the letters in my file, my heart ached over the thought of her wondering whether I'd loved her or if I'd given her away out of selfishness. I was worried she might be struggling with abandonment, anxiety, or depression because she didn't understand why her birth mother had not kept her close. I also hated that I couldn't offer her loving encouragement or even advice if she wanted it from me. Similarly, God wants to help us navigate this sin-broken world and to live in the light of our true identity as His children, loved and cherished! But we will remain in the darkness—which Oswald Chambers defined as "my own point of view, my prejudices and preconceived notions"—and prone to believe

> God wants to help us live in the light of our true identity as His children, loved and cherished! But we will remain in the dark and prone to believe untruths unless we diligently study His file of love letters to us.

---

[1] Oswald Chambers, *Still Higher for His Highest* (Grand Rapids: Zondervan, 1970), 110.

untruths unless we open and diligently study His file of love letters to us.[2]

God wants to be a blessing in the lives of each of His children. He wants to offer us the gifts that come with belonging to Him with all that we are: guidance from His Word, the Holy Spirit's comfort, and exciting insights into what will be our heavenly home. But all too often we Christians settle for knowing God at a polite distance. It's time to invite Him to be a *regular* part of our lives. And to do that, we must come to value His Word as the treasure trove it is!

And as surely as the exchange of files and letters helped Twila and me get to know one another better and prepare for our first meeting, so Bible reading and prayer deepen my relationship with God today and help prepare me for my first face-to-face meeting with Jesus in the future! Oh, how this fills me with eager and joyful anticipation for that grand reunion!

Looking back over my journey as a Christ-follower, I can now see that there were seasons of apathy toward God and it all stemmed from my lack of desire to seek Him in His Word. Apathy can ensnare even long-time believers if they allow other things to take priority over seeking God in His Word.

So many times in Scripture the Lord prompts us to seek Him. Yet this is not at all a selfish request. He knows what blessings are ours if we will actually seek Him. Consider those mentioned in just these few verses:

> 2 Chronicles 15:15: "They sought God eagerly, and he was found by them. So the Lord gave them rest on every side."

---

[2] Oswald Chambers, *The Oswald Chambers Daily Devotional Bible: 365 Daily Readings from the Author of* My Utmost for His Highest (Nashville: Thomas Nelson, 1993), 867 (see chap. 1, n. 4).

2 Chronicles 26:5: "As long as he sought the Lord, God gave him success."

2 Chronicles 30:18–19: "[King] Hezekiah prayed for them, saying 'May the Lord, who is good, pardon everyone who sets their heart on seeking God.'"

Psalm 24:5–6: "They will receive blessing from the Lord and vindication from God their Savior. Such is the generation of those who seek him."

Psalm 34:10: "The lions may grow weak and hungry, but those who seek the Lord lack no good thing."

Until we really begin to seek the Lord with wholehearted determination to know Him as well as possible this side of Heaven, we can only begin to fathom the blessings He wants to shower on us. God, our Creator, who loves us more than we are capable of loving our own children, desires to protect us and wants to see us enjoy life as He intended. It is in our best interest to learn as much as we can about Him and to strive to obey His commands given in the Bible. It is only in Him and in doing His will that our hearts find satisfaction.

To accurately gauge how much of a role seeking God has played in your spiritual life up to your opening this book, evaluate which of the following categories best represents your dominant attitude toward the Lord over the last six months.

(1) Pretend seekers are those Christians who say they want to seek God, yet do little more than attend church sometimes and send up a prayer in an emergency situation.

(2) Part-time seekers live what pastor and author A. W. Tozer

called the "half-way Christian life."[3] They genuinely desire to deepen their relationship with God, which is often evidenced by attending most church functions faithfully, reading biblically-based books like this one, and perhaps even going to Christian conferences. Spending daily time in the Word of God, however, often gets set aside as they focus on conquering life's responsibilities or checking other items (like nursery duty or giving or leading a small group) off their spiritual to-do lists.

(3) Persistent seekers have a true desire, even a drive, to diligently look for and honor God throughout their days. Each morning they rise with a need to know God better. Spending time with Him, in fact, is their top priority. They plan their schedules around daily alone time with God, and the Bible itself is their primary textbook.

Consider the psalmist's emphasis on the importance of God's Word to his own life. His writings express the heart of a persistent seeker:

> I seek you with all my heart;
>   do not let me stray from your commands.
> I have hidden your word in my heart
>   that I might not sin against you.
> [God,] I rejoice in following your statutes
>   as one rejoices in great riches.
> I meditate on your precepts
>   and consider your ways.
> I delight in your decrees;
>   I will not neglect your word. (Psalm 119:10–11, 14–16)

The psalmist follows God's Word, meditates on and considers it, and delights in and refuses to neglect it. To be able to honestly

---

[3] A. W. Tozer, Sept. 20 devotional, *Mornings with Tozer: Daily Devotional Readings* (Chicago: Moody Publishers, 2008), 31.

say, "I am seeking God," a believer needs to move beyond giving God mere nods of notice. She must even move beyond just reading or listening to the works of others who have sought Him. Rather, she must actively, continuously, and persistently express a real desire to know Him by thoroughly anchoring herself in Scripture. She must take it in and hide it in her heart. She must think of it as a crucial tool in growing her relationship with the Lord and in learning how to rightly approach life.

TOPICAL REFLECTIONS

1. What kind of seeker, as explained near the end of this chapter, best describes you in terms of your approach to God over the last few months? Would you say God is more likely grieved or pleased over your level of commitment to Him? Explain.

2. Review Psalm 119:10–11, 14–16 above. Focus on the verbs. What specific actions indicate that a person is serious about seeking God, about making Him the focus of life?

3. What did Anita do to convey her love to her daughter, to introduce herself to her? Explain how this parallels something God did for us.

4. How is your life different as a result of your being God's daughter through your faith in Christ? Be as specific as possible.

5. Hold your Bible in your hands and ponder the Oswald Chambers quote, "I hold in my hands the Thought of God." How does that make you think of the Bible differently?

CHAPTER 3

THE EXERCISE OUR SOULS NEED: PRAYER

"Although I have much to be grateful for as I look back over my life, I also have many regrets. I have failed many times, and I would do many things differently. . . . I would spend more time in spiritual nurture. . . . I would spend more time in prayer."[1]

– BILLY GRAHAM

SINCE THAT LIFE-CHANGING day when we met many years ago, I've continued to enjoy the amazing privilege of being in a wonderful relationship with my birth daughter, Twila. She and her children have made me a great-grandmother! While we've had our challenges in navigating our unique relationship, God has remained in the center of how we've handled them. Today we both feel nothing but gratitude for the way He brought healing out of our losses. He is so good!

What a gift it is to be able to talk with *all* my grown children! At this point in my life, I feel very blessed to be able to enjoy the sweet fellowship I find in keeping in touch with every one of them. Yet how often in the past I would go through prolonged

---

[1] Billy Graham, *Just As I Am: The Autobiography of Billy Graham* (New York: HarperCollins, 2007), 1253.

silences between me and the Lord, denying myself the same type of sweet conversation with Him! Having fellowshipped regularly with Him for many years now, I have to agree with Mother Teresa, who said, "The time we spend in having our daily audience with God is the most precious part of the day."[2] But I'd like to add to her comment: holding audience with Him doesn't have to be just a part of the day; it can extend from wake-up to bedtime.

I'll focus on that particular point—which is one of my favorites!—in a moment. For now, let me explain just how critical prayer is for one who desires to be a persistent God-seeker, who wants to experience the joy and peace that come with that. To be clear, I'm not talking about reciting prayers like "Now I lay me down to sleep ...," "God is great, God is good ...," or even Jesus's model prayer (see Matthew 6:9–13). Yes, they have their place, but the emphasis of this chapter involves speaking to God plainly and frankly, as you would talk to a close, respected friend during a heart-to-heart conversation.

To explain this idea, I'll start at Scripture's beginning. When God made Adam's body from the dust of the ground, His next act was to breathe "into his nostrils the breath of life." It was at that point that man "became a living being" (Genesis 2:7). People, then, are not just bodies; we are bodies with souls. The wonderful whole of Scripture explains that it isn't just believers' souls that will be with God forever one day; He will resurrect and upgrade our physical bodies too—as surely as He did Jesus's (see Philippians 3:20–21; 1 Corinthians 15:51–54)!

I bring up this body-and-soul dynamic here because it's easy for us to think of ourselves in terms of the physical and to neglect the spiritual. When we do that, it's also easy to assume prayer is an add-on, an unessential exercise. But I want to make the case that as surely as we wouldn't deprive our lungs of oxygen or our

---

[2] Mother Teresa, *In the Heart of the World: Thoughts, Stories & Prayers* (Novato, CA: New World Library, 2010), 102.

stomachs of the nourishment we need to stay healthy, we mustn't deprive our souls of what they need to work properly either.

The first thing the human soul needs to be truly healthy is a relationship with Jesus; after all, that's how we can be made right with God and know we have the hope of Heaven ahead. Jesus called Himself "the bread of life" (John 6:35) who gives us access to "the free gift of the water of life" (Revelation 22:17). In fact, in John 7:37 He said, "Let anyone who is thirsty come to me and drink." Anyone who accepts Christ is in position to experience eternal, abundant life: to have her spiritual hunger and thirst forever satisfied (see John 3:16; 10:10 NKJV; Psalm 107:9). Moreover, as we turn to God's Word for daily sustenance, we are prepped to thrive until the time comes for each of us to go Home. Maybe that's part of why Jesus said in Matthew 4:4, "Man shall not live on bread alone, but on every word that comes from the mouth of God." This passage also gets at my earlier point that feeding merely the body neglects the soul.

King David and the son of Korah expressed their personal experience of soul thirst when they wrote these words:

> You, God, are my God,
>   earnestly I seek you;
> I thirst for you,
>   my whole being longs for you,
> in a dry and parched land
>   where there is no water. (Psalm 63:1)
> As the deer pants for streams of water,
>   so my soul pants for you, my God.
> My soul thirsts for God, for the living God. (Psalm 42:1–2)

Looking ahead, these Old Testament-era men trusted in God's promised rescue plan, the Messiah, whom we know to be Christ. Therefore, what they ultimately thirsted for—and found through faith—was the same spiritual water we know: Jesus. In fact, Christ Himself explained that "rivers of living water" flow in every true believer because God's Holy Spirit takes up residence in them, quenching their thirst and—when they submit to His guidance—flowing through all they do (see John 7:37–39).[3]

So what does all this have to do with prayer? Conservative theologian Ole Hallesby said, "Prayer is the breath of the soul, the organ by which we receive Christ into our parched and withered hearts [anew].... As air enters in quietly when we breathe, and does its normal work in our lungs, so Jesus enters quietly into our hearts and does his blessed work there [when we pray]."[4] In other words, prayer is like a big spiritual inhale that allows all the goodness of God, His Word, and who we are as believers in Christ to really resonate in us.

> Prayer is like a big spiritual inhale that allows all the goodness of God, His Word, and who we are as believers in Christ to really resonate in us.

Like the oxygen we breathe, God's presence is with us all the time. In fact, we are surrounded by Him (Psalm 3:3). Yet we don't always feel God's presence any more than we are always conscious of the oxygen on which our bodies depend. Prayer brings the Lord to the forefront of our thoughts and clears our minds as surely as being hooked up to a can of oxygen helps someone struggling with altitude sickness find relief and renewed energy. Every time we cry out to God with prayer, we are acting in faith and opening the door for Him to come in and minister to our hearts again. We

---

[3] R. A. Torrey reminds us, "The Holy Spirit dwells in everyone who belongs to Christ (Romans 8:9). We may not have surrendered our lives utterly to this indwelling Spirit, we may be very far from being full of the Spirit, and we may be imperfect Christians. But if we have been born again, the Spirit dwells in us. What a glorious thought." R. A. Torrey, *God's Power in Your Life* (New Kensington, PA: Whitaker House, 2005), 162.

[4] Ole Hallesby, *Prayer: Expanded Edition* (Minneapolis: Augsburg Books, 1994), 14.

are showing the Lord that we realize our desperate dependence on Him.

Maybe you read these points about prayer and feel uneasy. In your mind, prayer is work. It's getting on your knees by your bed, awkwardly groping for something to say, and wondering whether you are doing a decent-enough job of it that the Lord pays attention. That's certainly how I felt about prayer early on.

But as I have journeyed on in my faith, I have come to understand that prayer is just speaking to God plainly and frankly, as you would speak to a close, respected friend during a heart-to-heart conversation. It doesn't have to be done in a certain posture, and it doesn't have to be eloquent.

Reading through the Bible, one finds simple, heartfelt prayers from everyday people in need of help. Consider these sample prayers. Note the subject matter of each as well as their different tones:

> In 2 Kings 6:17 Elisha simply prayed, "Lord, . . . open his eyes that he may see" (NKJV).

> In 2 Kings 19:15–16 King Hezekiah prayed with confident expectation: "Lord, the God of Israel, enthroned between the cherubim, you alone are God over all the kingdoms of the earth. You have made heaven and earth. Give ear, Lord, and hear; open your eyes, Lord, and see; listen to the words [our enemy] Sennacherib has sent to ridicule the living God."

> In Jonah 4:2 the reluctant prophet prayed rather grumpily: "Isn't this what I said, Lord, when I was still at home? That is what I tried to forestall by fleeing to Tarshish. I knew that you are a gracious and compassionate God,

slow to anger and abounding in love, a God who relents from sending calamity."

In Habakkuk 3:2 that prophet—like the psalmists—prayed poetically: "Lord, I have heard of your fame; I stand in awe of your deeds, Lord. Repeat them in our day, in our time make them known; in wrath remember mercy."

Later, in Jesus's parable of Luke 18:9–14, a tax collector prayed in a very blunt, sorrowful, straightforward manner: "God, have mercy on me, a sinner!"

And in Luke 23:42 the thief on the cross had little energy to spare, so he prayed simply: "Jesus, remember me." (This is an approach I find myself using often!)

All these men approached the Creator about very real and present situations they faced and concerns they had. None of them went to the Lord with empty recitations or formulas. And there's nothing in the passages to suggest that any of them were kneeling beside their beds as they prayed, doing so at a particular time of day—though there's nothing wrong with that. Rather, each man chose to speak to the Lord right where he was, in light of the moment.

Let's consider this from a different angle.

Have you ever walked through a large airport and noticed how nearly everybody is on a cell phone, many of them either talking to or texting loved ones or coworkers as they go about their travels? We live in an age when people can stay connected to family and friends easily, even when separated by hundreds of miles. But let's say that when I travel, which is often, I take a different approach to checking in with my husband, Paul. Though we both have cell phones and he loves to hear from me, I never call him until I have access to my hotel's landline and can talk to him on it as I kneel beside my hotel bed. In the back of my mind, I know Paul is always just a phone call away when I have a question or a problem or need his wisdom, but I hold off on talking to him until I am in place, until everything seems just right and I can really concentrate on my precise words. Would my determination to stick to a formula deepen our connection or work against it?

I'm sure you'll agree that a better approach to staying in touch with my husband involves being more spontaneous, talking to him more often as things come up, and sending him texts now and then just to tell him I'm thinking about him. That kind of activity will help us stay connected at the heart; it also reminds me not to take him for granted and allows him opportunity to help me navigate my days.

This is representative of the kind of communication the Lord desires to have with us. As surely as He wants us to pick up our Bibles regularly so He can speak to us through them, He wants us to pray without ever really stopping: from the moment we wake in the morning, at many points throughout our days, and even as we fall asleep at night. In light of that, I get up in the morning and "call" Jesus. We connect right away. And just as importantly, I never really hang up. True, in the old days I'd say a little prayer with a meal or by my bed at day's close or even as really big things came up in my life and think that was enough. I'd just hang up and move on with my day after those little pit stops, not thinking about God again until the next time. My unspoken attitude, I now see, was that I could handle the rest of the day by myself. And that took a terrible toll on my relationship with God. It left me with a nagging sense of disconnect.

One thing I've learned to do over the years is to think of prayer as something that is meant to be a constant, like breathing. It's a conversation that's never done. The apostle Paul said to "pray in the Spirit on all occasions" (Ephesians 6:18) and to "pray continually" (1 Thessalonians 5:17), and Jesus told His disciples that "they should always pray" (Luke 18:1).

A Helpful Tool for Keeping the Communication Lines Open

Sending up what I call my "MBM prayers," or moment-by-moment prayers, has proved really helpful in practicing this idea of keeping up ongoing communication with God. And I can testify that it has a huge payoff in my life and even my marriage.

Let me explain how MBM prayers work through a personal example. Keep in mind that the story I'm about to share with you began with my waking up to tell the Lord, "Good morning!" and inviting Him to help me live in a way pleasing to Him.

At some point by that early afternoon, however, Paul and I got into a big argument about something. Though I honestly can't remember anymore what the argument was about, I got so angry that I didn't want to talk to Paul. I certainly didn't want to get him the glass of water he asked me to bring him as he worked in our home office.

When he made that request, I said nothing aloud because nothing I said would've been very nice just then. But in my heart I sent up an MBM prayer: "Lord, I am so mad I want to scream. The last thing I want to do is get him a glass of water! But will You please help me to act lovingly by getting him what he wants anyway? I know from Your Word that it pleases You when we serve one another."

It made me feel a little better to know I'd been so honest with God, and I was able, by His grace, to get to the kitchen and fill a glass. Yet as I turned to take it to the office, a fresh wave of thinking about how angry I was made me want to slam the glass down onto the counter. So I sent up another MBM prayer: "You gotta help me. You gotta help me, God. Help me!"

I finally made it back to the office with a measure of calm. But then I saw Paul sitting there at his desk, looking unruffled, unfazed that our argument had not been officially settled, unaware of how hard it had been for me to go and get him the offering I carried. Suddenly I wanted nothing more than to dump the water all over his head!

For a split second I paused where I stood and my grip on the glass tightened. But once again I silently cried out with an MBM prayer. "Oh, Father, help me! I know it is not Your will for me to disrespect Paul. Please, please help me keep my mouth shut and just set this down beside him."

Praise God—He gave me the victory! I gently set the glass beside my husband without a word. Then out the door I went, grateful I did not give in to the heat of the moment and say words I would later regret.

This idea of sending up MBM prayers has proven really freeing to me over the years. It's my default approach to prayer anymore, seeing me through many family situations and unexpected interruptions in my day and even helping me cope with the unique stresses I face as I serve God through my JoyShop travels.[5]

Embracing Simplicity

In this era when we can hear TV preachers and seasoned radio personalities praying aloud every day of the week if we care to tune in, it really is easy to forget that prayer is just a simple plea for our loving Father's help. And it really doesn't have to be eloquent, though it can be, or wordy either. In fact, Jesus said, "When you pray, do not keep on babbling like pagans, for they think they will be heard because of their many words" (Matthew 6:7). The Lord hears His children the second they call.

---

[5] JoyShop is the name of my ministry. It started as a workshop designed to help people find joy through the blessing of a structured daily quiet time with God and has grown to include this resource. How I love to see people find joy as they practice the principles in this book!

The Lord reminded me of this one lazy afternoon when I was out in our family pool, floating around with one of my daughters. We were enjoying a Sabbath break when one of my sons came out the back door all dressed in his dirt-bike riding gear. When I asked what he was up to, he said he wanted to get some riding in on the trail next to our house. As he headed down the deck steps, I yelled, "Be careful!" Nevertheless, not ten minutes passed before I heard his faint but unmistakable cry: *"Help!"*

That one word sent me flying out of that pool at a full run to his side.

It turned out, thank the Lord, that he had injured only his tailbone, so his sister and I were able to walk him to the house between us. As we did, God used the situation to challenge my heart. My son had not had to theatrically yell out, "Oh, mighty wonderful Mother, if you promise to just come to my side to help me this one time I will dedicate my life to do everything you want henceforth!" Rather, he had called out one single and somewhat desperate-sounding *"Help!"* That's all it had taken for me to rush to him.

Psalm 18:6 similarly says, "In my distress I called to the Lord; I cried to my God for help." Verses 16 and 19 explain what God did in response to that desperate plea and why: "He reached down from on high and took hold of me.... He brought me out into a spacious place; he rescued me because he delighted in me."

The Lord, I think, truly appreciates it when we turn to Him in regular prayer, when we seek His help as humbly as my son called out for mine. After all, He *delights* in His children.

The Wise Choice or the Foolish One?

Since much of this book focuses on seeking spiritual nourishment through daily interaction with the bread of God's Word, I won't talk about how spiritually unhealthy we can become when we neglect to do that. I'm hopeful that if you were starving yourself that way when you first picked up this book, you are already working on correcting the problem as you engage with the Bible texts I include.

But suppose I tell you I've decided I'm expending a little too much effort on the whole breathing thing. Then I announce my plan that from this day forward I will breathe only occasionally, hold my breath as long as I can, and then breathe again only when I get desperate. I am sure you'd say something like "Anita, that would never work. You can't deprive yourself of oxygen that way!"

Set aside the idea that it would be medically impossible to pull that off for long. Can you imagine what I would look like, how I would feel, if I actually did that?

Yet this is essentially what Christians do when they treat prayer as anything less than the spiritual lifeline it is. They might wonder where God is, feel alone, and suspect He isn't worthy of their trust, yet all along the problem is not with Him. The problem is that they are refusing to breathe Him in with any sort of constancy and are suffering the natural consequences. Proverbs 19:3 seems appropriate here: "The foolishness of a man twists his [own] way, And his heart frets against the Lord" (NKJV).

South African pastor Andrew Murray put it this way:

> It is the lack of private prayer ... that explains the weakness in the Christian life. No wonder we can't resist the world. No wonder we fail to bring forth fruit abundantly. Nothing can change this except restoring the quiet time with the Lord in the life of a believer. We must ... daily sink our roots deeper into Christ and ... make the secret personal fellowship with God our priority. Then true godliness will flourish.[6]

---

[6] Andrew Murray, *The Inner Chamber: A Call to Daily Communion with Christ* (Sheffield, UK: CLC Publications, 2009), n.p. Kindle.

Allow me to get to the hardest truth of the matter. If you are only snacking on God's Word on Sunday mornings during preaching and are praying (think "breathing Christ in") only now and then, you are suffering spiritually. And while you might assume you are coasting along just fine, assuring yourself that all is well even if you're not experiencing the joy and peace you'd prefer, please consider that nonbelievers you might be trying to point to Christ are likely turned off by your poor spiritual health. In fact, it's highly unlikely they are seeing any real spiritual life in you, anything that would make them want what you have. Though a child of the King, you are settling for mediocrity at best and are suffering for it. And if you truly love Jesus with all your heart, soul, mind, and strength, you cannot be okay with that.

(Any discomfort you felt as you read that last paragraph, by the way, is a wonderful sign. Conviction is one of God's favorite tools for prompting us to get back on track.)

Built-in Mechanisms Calling Us to Prayer

As surely as our stomachs will growl should we go without food for long, God has built in several mechanisms to help us sense and hopefully subsequently feed our need to spend time with Him. The first is a feeling of *dissatisfaction*.

Look at this passage from Haggai: "You have planted much, but harvested little. You eat, but never have enough. You drink, but never have your fill. You put on clothes, but are not warm. You earn wages, but only to put them in a purse with holes in it. . . . Give careful thought to your ways" (Haggai 1:6–7).

In the original context of that verse, the Lord was calling the Jews of Haggai's day to finish rebuilding the temple, to get down to the business of prioritizing Him. He helped them see that all the other things to which they'd been giving their focus weren't satisfying them as He would. Likewise, we sometimes need a reminder that no matter how many possessions we gather or how much money we make or what measure of popularity we gain for ourselves, nothing but closeness with the Lord will ever truly satisfy us. "There is," Oswald Chambers commented, "only One Being who can satisfy the aching abyss of the human heart."[7] That Being is God, who loves to hear from us. Sometimes it takes realizing that all our stuff is failing to deliver to get us to pray. That, in fact, is part of what led me to cry out to God in the way I describe in this book's introduction.

Another mechanism God uses to help us see and feel our need to spend time fellowshipping with Him in prayer and Scripture study is *loneliness*. Have you ever noticed that even in a room full of people, a wave of "I feel so alone" can come over you? I have, and for a long time I thought there was something wrong with me because of it. Then I came across this quote by Hubert Van Zeller: "The soul hardly ever realizes it, but whether he is a believer or not, his loneliness is really homesickness for God."[8] Reading that made me realize that God will sometimes allow me to get lonely—even in a crowd!—because He wants that feeling to drive me to talk to Him, to remember that He is always by my side, waiting to be welcomed into every part of my day, into every situation. When I live in light of that, I never have to be lonely—no matter what. I just speak to God—which is what loneliness calls me to do.

The next built-in mechanism God gives people that should motivate us to spend time talking with Him is *restlessness*, that uneasy and fitful feeling you get that keeps you from being able to relax. Noting this personally was what led Saint Augustine to say, "Thou hast made us for thyself, O Lord, and our heart is restless until it rests in thee."[9] It was no coincidence that Jesus said, "Come

---

[7] Oswald Chambers, quoted in David MacCasland, ed., *The Quotable Oswald Chambers* (Grand Rapids: Discovery House Publishers, 2011), n.p. Kindle.

[8] Martin H. Manser, ed., *The Westminster Collection of Christian Quotations* (Louisville, KY: Westminster John Knox Press, 2001), 233.

[9] Saint Augustine, quoted in Susan Shumsky, *How to Hear the Voice of God* (Newburyport, MA: New Page Books, 2008), 28.

to me . . . and I will give you rest" (Matthew 11:28). As Augustine theorized, the answer to our restlessness issue really is solved when we take matters to the Lord. Those who don't know Him can find salvation, and they can then be comforted and motivated by the assurances and purposefulness that He offers His people.

Unfortunately, though, we often try to cope with restlessness in one of two ways. We either stay too busy to let ourselves feel it or we turn to something like social media, television, online gaming, or even alcohol to take our minds off it. Anytime we find ourselves self-soothing with unnecessary busyness or meaningless activity, we should ask ourselves why we aren't instead turning to God. If every time we had an urge to check our social media accounts or to numb out by watching hours of TV we'd opt to seek God in prayer or open our Bibles and read His Word instead, we just might be surprised to find ourselves feeling much more contented.

> Anytime we find ourselves self-soothing with unnecessary busyness or meaningless activity, we should ask ourselves why we aren't instead turning to God.

Another divinely built-in mechanism designed to motivate us to seek God in prayer and Scripture study is *weakness*. I'm not talking about the kind of weakness evidenced by flabby arms or not being able to open a pickle jar. I'm talking about spiritual weakness, a propensity to cave into temptations easily.

Disciples Peter, James, and John illustrated this concept for us when they just couldn't keep their eyes open to keep watch with Jesus just before He was arrested (see Matthew 26:36–45). Peter highlighted the power of weakness again when a little later he got so scared that he denied even knowing Jesus (see Matthew 26:69–75). I see weakness in myself when I become so self-focused that things have got to be my way or no one's way—like when I'm playing a card game of Rook and get so competitive about it that

I no longer care whether the other players are enjoying it, or when my plans don't pan out like I want and I turn into an irritable grump. You might see it in yourself when an emotional trigger gets pulled and you immediately spew hurtful or foul words or once again turn to an addictive substance. In Matthew 26:41 Jesus said, "Watch and pray so that you will not fall." On any point that we recognize weakness in ourselves, we need to get to praying. It's what weakness prompts us to do. Every weakness that arises, in fact, is an opportunity to exercise dependence on God.

One final built-in mechanism that calls us to prayer is painful *brokenness*. C. S. Lewis said, "Pain is God's megaphone to get our attention, and it's in the pain that we discover our desire for God."[10] Too often, though, we allow brokenness itself to become our focus. We beg and plead for God to remove our hurts immediately, as if they are somehow in the way of our ability to move forward with Him confidently. But all of our hurt serves as an important reminder: We really can't just sail through life on this sin-cursed planet. We *need God* moment by moment! So let's choose to allow every hurt to make us call out to Him in dependence and trust because He is more than enough to meet all our needs in our brokenness.

It's in our dissatisfaction, loneliness, restlessness, weakness, and painful brokenness that we are most effectively reminded to seek God in prayer. Could it be that keeping up ongoing conversations with God might spare us the need for so many reminders?

Please take a few moments to talk to the Lord about whatever is going on in your life. It doesn't have to be fancy or long. Just speak with the knowledge that hearing from you pleases Him.

---

[10] C. S. Lewis, quoted in Larry Crabb, *Shattered Dreams: God's Unexpected Path to Joy* (Colorado Springs: Waterbrook Press, 2011), 91.

TOPICAL REFLECTIONS

1. Consider that you have a dual nature: you are both a physical body and a soul. Which part of yourself do you spend the most time caring for? Why do you think most people tend to give the physical aspect the most attention?

2. Does thinking of Jesus as the Bread of Life motivate you to pray? Why or why not?

3. Read 1 Thessalonians 5:16–18. What does this reveal about God's will for every believer?

4. Dissatisfaction, loneliness, restlessness, weakness, and brokenness can all indicate we are depriving ourselves of spending enough time with God in prayer and Bible reading. Which indicator have you seen show up in your life? Share about a time when you addressed it by focusing on something other than Him. How did that work out?

5. Basing your answer on your spiritual communication habits alone, how good a job do you think you are doing at conveying your love for and interest in God? How well are you trusting in His ability to hear you?

PART 2:

Practical Suggestions for Seeking Faithfully

CHAPTER 4

START EACH DAY THE RIGHT WAY

"Do not have your concert first, then tune your instrument afterwards. Begin the day with the Word of God and prayer and get first of all in harmony with Him."[1]
– Hudson Taylor

FOR MUCH OF my adult life, I struggled with showing up to meet with God in any consistent way. In all honesty, I would meet with God when and where it suited me. And since I want to be transparent here, I even lacked the enthusiasm one might expect a girl to have when she grasps who she's getting to meet with: our Creator God! Yet somehow, by the grace of God, He nevertheless helped me realize I needed to come up with a disciplined plan and put it into practice if I was going to have success in growing in my relationship with Him!

For me the most effective plan is a structured morning quiet time. I decided on this approach in part because I took Matthew 6:33, where Jesus said to "seek *first* [God's] kingdom" (emphasis

---

[1] William Revell Moody, ed., *Record of Christian Work* (East Northfield, MA: Record of Christian Work Company, 1910), 59.

mine), as a literal cue. Over time I discovered that these simple disciplines helped me to stay consistent in seeking to grow daily in my relationship with Jesus. As I began to teach these basic reminders to others, many confirmed and shared with me that they too had found it to be an excellent tool for actively prioritizing God daily and for the long haul.

If you desire to go from a part-time seeker to a persistent seeker of God, the following simple steps, listed in the next section, will help you get started on a new life-giving adventure. You too will come to a greater understanding of this truth spoken by A. W. Tozer: "To seek God does not narrow one's life, rather it brings it to the level of highest possible fulfillment."[2] But it all begins with a commitment.[3]

Commit to the Task of Setting Your Heart on the Lord

In 1 Peter 3:15 Christ-followers are told, "In your hearts set Christ apart [as holy—acknowledging Him, giving Him first place in your lives] as Lord" (AMP). A look in the dictionary reveals that to set something apart requires being "determined in advance" to do so, to be "prepared for action" on a matter.[4]

If you think about it, you probably set your heart on things all the time. I know my personality is such that when I see something I want, I'm determined to go after it! For instance, when my kids were little, I set my heart on a little quiet time alone with the television each day. I was determined to watch *General Hospital*,

---

[2] A. W. Tozer, *The Pursuit of God with Study Guide: The Human Thirst for the Divine* (Chicago: Moody, 2006), n.p. Kindle.

[3] Should you find yourself unable to begin your day in the Word, please adjust the advice and steps advocated to suit your situation. The underlying goal here is being intentional and consistent about spending time with Jesus. We are assured, "There is now no condemnation for those who are in [Him]" (Romans 8:1). And as one author wisely expressed, "It's not the accuracy of your seeking but the yearning of your heart that moves the Father.... [I]t's your yearning for Him that He loves and honors." S. J. Hill, *Enjoying God: Experiencing Intimacy with the Heavenly Father* (Lake Mary, FL: Charisma Media, 2001), 141.

[4] *The Oxford American Desk Dictionary: Major New Edition*, s.v. "set" (Oxford, UK: Oxford University Press, 1998), 548.

and I aligned my kids' meals and naps so that I had the living room all to myself when it came on. More recently, when I determined I needed to eat better, I knew I'd struggle when I got to the grocery store and all its tasty but terrible-for-me temptations. So I set my heart on bringing only healthy food choices like lean meat and low-calorie snacks into our home as well as ordering fresh produce from our market stand. I had to make careful meal plans and lists ahead of time. Then from the moment I entered the store, I avoided so much as looking at my favorite snacks. My heart was *set* on changing my eating habits.

Similarly, truly setting our hearts on Christ means work, foresight. It takes intentionality and determination. The great news is that the Holy Spirit is a wonderful help to us in the effort, and He extends lavish grace to us along the way. When we are determined to set our love upon Him, He will help us with developing the discipline to make room for Him in our days! As a starting place, I'd like to share five practical steps toward getting a day off on the right foot that have encouraged and grown me in the faith as I've made them a part of regular practice. I offer these steps geared toward a successful quiet time here in the hope that they'll aid you in the effort of fully setting your heart on Him too.

1. Make the decision that as surely as you will wake in the morning to dress, eat breakfast, and get to work on time, you will meet with God.
This first step does not refer to an "I've already done that" decision. In fact, should you find yourself thinking, *I've already tried a start-the-day-with-God plan only to see it fail*, put that incident behind you—it's time to start fresh! What I'm advocating here is a regular, conscious choice as you lay your head on the pillow each night. Every evening you must decide that the important work of spending time with the Lord in the morning is a mission-critical part of your day. Make up your mind that as surely as you wouldn't go to

the office without taming your pillow-wild hair, you don't want to face whatever the day holds without first spending time with God.

Then, when your alarm sounds in the morning, remind yourself of this decision. Yes, you need to throw back the covers and get up and around because showing up is half the battle! But you also need to take a spiritual stand. In the book of Joshua, the Israelites' new leader gives the people this charge: "Choose for yourselves this day whom you will serve. . . . [A]s for me and my household, we will serve the Lord" (Joshua 24:15). By the time your feet hit the floor, choose who is going to be in charge of the next twenty-four hours. We often hear the admonishment to make Jesus Christ the Lord of our lives. But if we can't make Him Lord of each day, He'll never really be Lord of our entire existence. As I've heard Bible teacher Beth Moore say, "A victorious day begins with a victorious morning."

> If we can't make Him Lord of each day, He'll never really be Lord of our entire existence.

Establishing God on the throne of our lives really does begin with small decisions like *I'm gonna get up to spend time with Him.*

2. *Pray for a fresh desire for God and His Word.*

With the idea that God is to be an essential part of your morning firmly settled, you are ready for step two of getting a day off on the right spiritual footing. Whether you do this next part while putting on your robe and slippers, while brushing your teeth, or while showering, pray and ask God to give you a true desire to meet with Him before you launch into your other responsibilities. Our goal is to want to spend regular time with God not out of a gritty determination to do so but out of a heart of love that desires to honor Him with an attitude that's submissive to His will and welcoming of His influence. As Andrew Murray said in a devotional entry that speaks to my heart, "You can be certain that God greatly desires that you should live in this intimate fellowship with Him. He will, in answer to your prayer, enable you to do so."[5]

Even now, after years of faithfully practicing a morning quiet time with the Lord, I start my days this way. I usually say something like this: "God, give me a fresh desire to really want to know You more. I'm tired. I've got a lot going on today. But please know I'm choosing to nourish my soul with Your written Word because I love You." In Matthew 7:7 Jesus said, "Ask and it will be given to you." I can testify that this is a prayer God generously answers every time I pray it sincerely.

3. Go to your special place to meet with God, and make sure you get there on time.

The third step to getting the day headed in the right direction involves a lot of discipline. I'll start with the lighter half of this discussion before I get to the hard part.

For years I held my daily quiet time randomly, at various spots throughout our home. Frankly, I met God wherever it was most convenient: at the kitchen table, on the couch, still in my bed. But there came a day when I sensed that doing so felt a little too informal. And it was a pain and very distracting to have to hunt down my Bible each time. When I prayed about the matter, I suddenly pictured the way I'd go to meet a friend at a local coffee shop where we would talk and enjoy fellowship in a setting dedicated to such encounters. And that's when I realized that I really should find a place in my house that could become my "spot" to fellowship with God . . . kind of like a favorite date locale, if you will.

After thinking about it, I decided the big upholstered chair in my living room was the best place to meet with God every morning. Since then, I've sat in it so consistently for that purpose that the chair is wearing out! But I don't mind. You see, that chair has

---

[5] Andrew Murray, *365 Daily Devotions on Prayer* (Uhrichsville, OH: Barbour Publishing, 2013), 241.

become a sacred space, a place where I seek and sometimes even sense the very presence of my Father. In fact, I've come to think of it as my physical place of refuge that never ceases to remind me of my ultimate Refuge (see Psalm 46:1; 62:7–8).

Consider your options when it comes to where you can meet with the Lord. Do you have a favorite chair? A cozy spot on the floor of your closet? A window seat? Where's the best place in your home that you can go each day for a little alone time with God? Deciding on that now will eliminate one possible distraction as the hour of quiet time approaches.[6]

Now it's time for the less pleasant part of this third step: we need to show up...to be in our spots—wherever they are—promptly.

Initially, I didn't think it was too big of a deal to have a predetermined quiet time slot each day. I went about the whole meeting-with-the-Lord idea with a lot of flex: sometimes I'd have quiet time before the kids got up. Sometimes I'd have it after they were off to school. And honestly, there were days when I didn't have it at all. But then such exceptions got to be so common that I realized that if I didn't start my day with a set period of fellowship with Jesus, then my quiet time was likely not to happen—at least, not as anything but a rushed afterthought that missed the whole point. So I determined I'd be in my chair promptly at a certain quarter hour each morning. Having that specific time on my mental radar was a game-changer for me.

Yet on the weekends, when the kids were off their school schedule, I tended to go off mine. In fact, I'd sometimes sleep right through the part of the hour I usually would've spent in my chair! For a long time I just told myself it wasn't a big deal. I rationalized that I needed the rest. But then I started encountering Bible verses that challenged me to rethink.

Ephesians 5:14 says, "Wake up, sleeper, rise from the dead,

---

[6] Even when I travel, I make a point to search out what will be my morning "spot" while I stay at a certain location. Vacations do not interfere with my spending daily time with God.

and Christ will shine on you." That made me wonder if while I was dead to the world under my sheets, I was missing out on having Christ shine new truths from His Word into my life. That seemed a tragic waste!

Proverbs 26:14 says, "As a door turns on its hinges, so a sluggard turns on his bed." That certainly made my eyebrows rise. When it comes to growing in my relationship with Jesus, I do not want to be labeled a sluggard! In fact, I don't want to be called that in any context.

Second Chronicles 16:9 says, "The eyes of the Lord range throughout the earth to strengthen those whose hearts are fully committed to him." That reminded me that God is looking for hearts sold out to Him. And it was just possible that in sleeping through our usual time together, I was sending Him the message that mine really wasn't.

And finally, in Hebrews 12:1 Paul says, "Let us throw off everything that hinders and the sin that so easily entangles. And let us run with perseverance the race marked out for us." That one helped me see that in my spiritual run alongside Jesus, one of the biggest hindrances to my feeling close with Him came down to my unwillingness to "throw off" my bed-blankets in the morning!

Perhaps about now you're feeling a little uncomfortable over my emphasis on believers rising early in pursuit of spiritual nourishment and to honor God. You know I'm about to urge you to start setting your alarm a few minutes earlier so you can spend time with Jesus at your day's open, and that's a little alarming on its own. *You don't know what my morning is like, Anita!* you might think. *I barely get enough sleep as it is! I don't have time for that!* If these are your thoughts, please know I'm not insisting on this as a rule. Rather, I'm extending what I've seen for myself to be a helpful invitation, one that it seems even Jesus Himself would've embraced given His approach to ministry (see Mark 1:35). I'm urging you to simply try living out the wisdom found in passages like those above and in so many others, like Psalm 63:1. It says, "You, God, are my God, earnestly I seek you." The Hebrew word for *earnestly* is *shachar*, which means "to look early or diligently for."[7] That word *earnestly* refers to going about a thing with deep, sincere feeling. So please consider this: if a person in our busy culture really intends to seek God earnestly, isn't choosing a specific time to meet with Him and setting an alarm to do so a great combo step in the right direction?

I realize that what I'm asking is not an easy task—at least it's not easy for everyone. Moreover, some have legitimate reasons to choose to commune with God at later points in the day, and I cheer them in their efforts. But what I am after here is spurring you on to giving this particular seeking method a sincere try.

So think about it. Will you, starting tomorrow, attempt to show up at your spot at a set time? And if the answer is yes, what time will that be? Will this require setting your alarm clock—which I prefer to think of as an "opportunity clock"—a little differently? Ordering your morning a little differently? Mentally work through those matters now.

Before moving forward, I'd like to offer a word of encouragement. Should you follow steps one through three, making it to your chosen spot of fellowship with God on time—only to doze off with your Bible in your lap once you get there—the Lord just might smile anyway. The Father may well look over at Jesus and say, "Would you look at that, Son? She loves Us enough to show up! She made the effort to get here." And Jesus may glance up from watching you to say, "Yes, Father. Isn't it *beautiful*?"

4. Set a timer.

One small step I took in the beginning was to set the timer on my microwave for twenty to thirty minutes right after I made my

---

[7] Robert L. Thomas, ed., *The New American Standard Exhaustive Concordance of the Bible: Including Hebrew-Aramaic and Greek Dictionaries* (Nashville: B&H Publishing Group, 1981), 1604.

pot of coffee. I found this very helpful in that I didn't have to keep checking my phone, which was a distraction. Instead, I could actually meet with Jesus with a relaxed attitude and enjoy that time, focusing on our friendship and growing to know Him more. When the timer beeped, then I knew it was time to wrap up.

It could be, though, that today the thought of spending just fifteen minutes doing something as simple as reading a passage of Scripture, reflecting on it, and speaking to the Lord about it and what's going on in your heart seems about as easy as walking across a canyon on a tightrope. And you can't imagine actually enjoying it. I once felt that way, yet now one of the most pleasurable activities of each day is relaxing and enjoying sitting with God and allowing myself the opportunity to hear Him speak to my heart! I can testify that each of these quotes holds true:

> "Every minute you seek God is a minute enriched with new life and new power from God."[8]
> – Francis Frangipane

> "The amount of time we spend with Jesus—meditating on His Word and His majesty, seeking His face—establishes our fruitfulness in the Kingdom."[9]
> – Charles Stanley

> "We may measure our growth in grace by the growth of our love for private Bible Study. . . . We should aim at securing at least half an hour each day for the leisurely and loving study of the Bible. To some this may seem

---

[8] Francis Frangipane, *Holiness, Truth, and the Presence of God: For Those Who Are Unsatisfied with Their Spiritual Life and Willing to Do Something about It* (Lake Mary, FL: Charisma House Publishing, 2011), 13.

[9] Charles Stanley, *How to Listen to God* (Nashville: Thomas Nelson, 2002), n.p. Kindle.

like a long time, but it will soon seem all too short. It is an appetite that grows as it is fed."[10]
– F. B. Meyer

In the event that your eyebrows shot up over the "half an hour" mentioned in that last quote, know that spending a whole thirty minutes or more with God each day is not a rule or goal written in concrete either. But I do think it's an admirable aim. As F. B. Meyer pointed out, "The Bible seldom speaks, and certainly never its deepest, sweetest words, to those who always read in a hurry."[11] If you don't allow for enough time to actually relax and enjoy God's presence, it may prove tough to hear from Him on a personal level. As surely as things go in one ear and out the other when my husband tries to tell me something as I hurry out the door, I'm not really giving God an opportunity to get through to me if I'm rushing through quiet time to get on with the rest of the day.

One great quote I can certainly relate to is this: "Five minutes with God and His Word is worth more than all the rest of the day."[12] I encourage you to give the Lord as large a window of time as you reasonably can.

5. *Structure your time.*

This is a good point at which to ask, why wait till the end of this book to get started with a structured quiet time? Indeed, you can begin anytime. Although in chapter 8 I'll provide you with a more formal routine to put into practice during each of your quiet times, I want to encourage you to start tomorrow with this very simple structured approach:

---

[10] Frederick Brotherton Meyer, *Steps into the Blessed Life* (Henry Altemus, 1896), 287.
[11] Ibid., 289.
[12] Oswald Chambers, quoted in David MacCasland, ed., *The Quotable Oswald Chambers* (Grand Rapids: Discovery House Publishers, 2011), n.p. Kindle (see chap. 3, n. 7).

1. With your timer set, begin by telling the Lord thank You for the opportunity to meet with Him, by asking Him to cleanse you of any unrepented sin, and by asking Him to teach you through His Word.
2. Then, depending on what day it is on your calendar, read a matching chapter of Proverbs. For instance, if tomorrow is February 18, read Proverbs 18. If July 1, read Proverbs 1. You can't go wrong on this since there are thirty-one chapters in that book. Many sayings you'll find there are simple and will stick in your mind easily.
3. Then read that day's chapter a second time, making note of the verse or verses that most stand(s) out to you. (Often it's through these verses that God speaks to a heart the most loudly.)
4. When you're done, write down in a Joy Journal (a notebook you'll keep with your Bible and pen) what drew you to certain verses. Jot down why they are resonating with you and how you think they might apply to a situation you face.
5. Then pray, thanking God for what you've read and asking Him to be Lord of your day.

By following even this super-simple structure at the start of your morning, you are preparing yourself for success. And I encourage you to begin employing it tomorrow. In fact, I'm excited about what you might gain in doing so!

Be Alert for Ways to Share What the Father Showed You During Quiet Time

One particularly amazing aspect of seeking God was not on my radar early on, but time and experience have revealed the blessings of actually telling others about who God is and what He reveals to me through His Word. In fact, it's a practice that's proven immensely helpful in learning just how good and involved in my life He really is. Moreover, it's a great way to participate in the Great Commission that Jesus gave to His followers: "Go and make disciples of all nations ... teaching them to obey everything I have commanded you" (Matthew 28:19–20). All of Christ's followers are to be His witnesses; we are to testify about who He is and what He's done (see Acts 1:8). We introduce the world to Jesus.

Honestly, though, I used to get uptight when I'd hear preachers urge me to do something along this line. Sharing my faith with other people seemed overwhelming, largely because I always felt inadequate. *I'm no pastor,* I'd think. *Those I try to talk to might know all about my past and decide I'm not holy enough to talk about Jesus.* Also quick to plague me were thoughts like these: *I'm not smart enough to be a witness for Christ! Wouldn't it be better to wait to share until I can answer every question about Him like well-known Bible scholars seem to do?*

Yet—praise God—when I actually decided to start taking the Lord up on His command to tell others about Him, I learned a few things. First, I don't have to share Him as a Bible scholar, and I don't have to share about Him as a preacher. And sharing Him really has nothing to do with smarts. It certainly isn't just for those with squeaky-clean pasts because the Bible (I'm thankful to say) includes God-loving characters who failed in one way or the other. It also makes it very clear that "all have sinned and fall short of the glory of God" and that without the blood of Christ covering the sins of those who trust in Him, "there is no one righteous, not even one" (Romans 3:23, 10). All I am asked to do is to talk about Jesus, what He has done in my life, and what He tells me in His Word to the best of my ability. And, praise God, I can do that just as I am! His Spirit will work through me as I open my mouth in obedience to His desire that I "declare the praises of him who called [me] out of darkness into his wonderful light" (1 Peter 2:9).

Maybe you read that and thought, *Sure, you can say that now,*

Anita! You travel around and speak about Jesus all the time. You've got this down! I'm just not ready to talk about my faith yet. I might embarrass myself, and I'm sure I wouldn't do it right! God can't really use me.

Let me tell you about a time not so long ago when I shared about Jesus from a place of total brokenness and unpreparedness, a time when all my love of speaking and any confidence I'd managed to gain on spiritual subjects totally failed me. I share this story because I want you to see that our wonderful God chose to work through me anyway. May it help you realize that He can also work through you, wherever you are in your journey.

A few years ago, my family went through a very difficult time. One of my kids was dealing with severe chronic depression, and the ongoing and asphyxiating anxiety of watching the battle just seemed to flip a switch in me. I felt physically broken. Paul suggested the two of us take a little vacation to try to soak up some sunshine, thinking that would help me reset. But once we got to Florida, I just started falling apart to a greater extent. I couldn't sleep at all; and in spite of the beautiful, warm days down there, I shook as uncontrollably as if I'd been out in the cold too long.

I called my doctor up in Pennsylvania, who prescribed a couple of medications based on my symptoms. The plan was for me to go in for an office visit once we returned home. Yet each subsequent day of the trip, I felt worse. Paul finally agreed to put me on a plane so I could go and see the doctor early; he knew, given my apparent distress, that it would be very difficult for me to make the long drive back to Pennsylvania in our pickup.

Once I boarded the flight we had scheduled, I weakly shuffled down the aisle of my plane to find there were two men sitting in my assigned row: one was in the center and the other man was in the aisle seat. Miserable as I felt, I sent up a small MBM prayer to praise the Lord that I'd have the seat by the window and that I could sit with men, who weren't nearly as likely to engage me in small talk as many women would be. With a little sigh, I soon situated myself in that seat and balled the comfort blanket I'd brought with me into a pillow. I tried to sleep with it propped between my head and the window as the plane took off. "Oh, God," I prayed silently, "just get me home."

Ninety minutes later, I'd still not slept a wink and felt so jittery I was sure I was about to make a scene that would shock my seatmates. I wanted to scream. I wanted to cry. I just wanted to feel like myself again. Not knowing what else to do, I finally looked at the man beside me and blurted, "I need to get up. Will you let me out?"

He nodded politely and both he and the passenger on the other side of him stood so I could walk past them to the aisle. Once there, I made my way to the aircraft's tiny restroom. I was relieved to find that it did help me to stand up and get my blood flowing, but I felt miserable all over again when I got back into my seat to realize there was still a whole half-hour's flight standing between me and home. "Oh, God," I prayed silently again, "*Please help me survive this endless trip!*"

The intensity I felt inside just seemed to grow from there. The walls, in fact, seemed to be drawing nearer. I felt like I was going to literally jump out of my skin! So after I'd been back in my seat for only a minute or two, I looked at the guy beside me and abruptly asked, "What's your name?"

"Joe," he replied with a cautious smile that said he was feeling a little worried about me, the jumpy stranger beside him.

"I'm Anita," I said. "And, Joe, I don't want to scare you, but I'm having problems. I really need you to talk to me. I need some distraction!"

Now, Joe might've been thinking, *Oh, great! I'm sitting beside a crazy woman!* However, he was nothing but gracious as he started telling me about his family and giving little insights into his life. I was so glad I'd asked for his help that I wanted to cry; indeed, he proved to be wonderful at getting my mind off things. By the time the pilot announced our arrival over Philadelphia's airport, I found myself wanting to thank him and lacking words. So I reached down into my purse to grab a copy of my personal teen pregnancy story that I hoped might bless him.

"Joe," I said hurriedly, "I don't know if you even want this. But I wrote a book, and I'd like you to have it in appreciation for your help today."

"What's it about?" he asked, reaching for it.

I froze, too weakened by whatever was going on with me to say anything, and sent up one more rather desperate MBM prayer: "Lord, please help me share my story and the parallel of Twila's file being like the love letter of Your Word one more time. May it speak into this man's life."

Then, with what I'm sure was the shortest and shakiest version I've ever given of my story, I replied to Joe's question. Both he and the man beside him listened intently as we made our final circles above the airport. When I finished, Joe thanked me politely and the man next to him said, "Hey—would you mind if I looked at that book?"

Joe handed it over and he gave it a quick perusal before focusing on the back cover. "Oh, I see you went to Messiah College," he said to me with a smile. "I went to Messiah!"

It turned out we had attended that school at the same time and even knew each other. Moreover, he was curious to learn more about my ministry.

I could barely reply to him, but I did the best I could as the plane lowered.

"You'll be okay," he said when we finally landed. "God will get you through."

I thanked him as people began standing to retrieve their overhead bags. Then Joe, with my book tucked under his arm, tried to help me feel better too. He asked, "Any chance you're going through menopause?"

My mouth must've dropped open at that because he hurried to say. "I'm sorry if that was rude. It's just that my wife acts like you sometimes!"

At that, I actually managed a little laugh and shrug, wondering why it had not occurred to me sooner that I might indeed be dealing with side effects of exactly what he'd mentioned.

"Thank you so much for talking me through these last thirty minutes," I said to the two men as we walked down the loading ramp together. "I believe God sent you to those very seats to help get me home, and I can't thank you enough."

The second man smiled and gave me a friendly wave before heading off to catch a connecting flight. Joe stuck close just long enough to tell me this: "You know, Anita, I'm a Catholic. But honestly, I only read my Bible about once a month, and only when I have to prepare for something. After hearing your story, though, well ... I feel like I want to open the Word more. Think I'll start a habit of actually praying with my family too. So thank you, Anita. And may God bless you and your ministry."

He soon walked away into the crowd, and into my mind popped this beautiful truth I'd read during one of my morning times with the Lord. The apostle Paul too had once struggled with some kind of malady that made him feel completely inadequate for the work the Lord had given him to accomplish. When he prayed about it, the Lord replied, "My grace is sufficient for you, for my power is made perfect in weakness." So Paul decided to "boast ... gladly about [his] weaknesses, so that Christ's power [might] rest on [him]." He said, "[F]or Christ's sake, I delight in weaknesses, ... in difficulties. For when I am weak, then I am strong" (2 Corinthians 12:9–10). How humbling it was to realize that God didn't even need me in my right mind to use me; He just wanted me willing to share what I could in that moment.

Friend, whatever God does in your life or teaches you in your quiet times, be willing to share it. Just speak what you can and allow the Holy Spirit to do His thing. God wants us to be faithful. He can do *amazing* things when we are.

The Lord speaks to us in the quiet moments of fellowship with Him not so we can keep His wonderful truths all to ourselves. He wants us to bless others by sharing them. And as we do, we are refreshed, others are encouraged, and Jesus receives honor.

Count and Be Willing to Pay the Cost
I want to be used by God to help make sure that many, many more people come to trust in Jesus as Lord and to grow in the faith. That, I know, is where the life purpose of every child of God is ultimately found. But living that out involves ongoing surrender, a willingness to spend daily time in pursuit of the Lord as well as a willingness to pour our time and our talents He has so graciously given us into the lives of others.

Maybe as you think about adopting the kind of changes I suggest in this chapter, you still sense a little resistance down in your heart. You aren't sure you can talk yourself into paying the time cost I'm encouraging or just aren't certain you'll ever be ready to invest in others by obediently sharing your faith. All of it still feels uncomfortable, scary. If so, I hope you'll be inspired by the following true stories of people who faced their fears. Each, I am confident, is today living out a reward in Heaven that is so great they would heartily encourage us not to hesitate to seek God and to do wholeheartedly *whatever* He wants of us.

Our brother in the faith William Tyndale had a deep desire to get the Bible printed into English, a language the common people could understand. But the corrupt European church of Tyndale's day felt that commoners like us should leave Bible study to the clergy. It was read to the people only in Latin, which few could comprehend, and the false teachers of Tyndale's day were heartily opposed to ever changing that. Tyndale knew beyond doubt that God's Word is spiritual food for all His people and that he was supposed to help get it into their hands, so he not only painstakingly translated and printed an English Bible but also smuggled precious copies of it into England. The man lived in terrible poverty, exile, hunger, and general suffering because his work was so opposed. In fact, he was burned at the stake on October 6, 1536.[13] Yet today you and I enjoy having Bibles of our own largely because of this faithful man.

Joan Waste, a blind woman born about the time Tyndale died, wanted a New Testament she could understand more than anything. She saved all her money to buy one but then had to find and pay people to read it to her. This woman spent great amounts of time memorizing Scripture, seeking to hide it in her heart so she could better live in a way pleasing to God. But as she did so, Waste quickly grew aware that indeed the Catholic Church of that day had been withholding truth from the people and teaching false doctrines—such as the idea that the Communion Supper somehow turns into the real blood and flesh of Jesus and that people can buy their way out of hell and so sidestep the need for Christ. For making such breaks with Scripture known and choosing to live in light of them, Joan was arrested. Her brother held her hand as she was led to the stake to be burned alive at the age of twenty-two. Nearly five hundred years later, we—this humble woman's family in the faith—are still talking about and inspired by her.[14]

Theologian Urban T. Holmes III theorized, "A life incapable of significant sacrifice is also incapable of courageous action."[15] Hudson Taylor, a great missionary to China, said this: "An easy-going, non-self-denying life will never be one of power."[16] I include all of this to say that if you want the power of God in your life, it's

---

[13] Henry Hampton Halley, *Halley's Bible Handbook* (Grand Rapids: Zondervan, 1962), 754. Also, see the Wikipedia article on William Tyndale: https://en.wikipedia.org/wiki/William_Tyndale.

[14] Joan's story appears in *Foxe's Book of Martyrs* (Newbury, FL: Bridge-Logos, 2001), n.p. Kindle. See also the Wikipedia article on Joan Waste: https://en.wikipedia.org/wiki/Joan_Waste.

[15] Urban T. Holmes III, *Spirituality for Ministry* (Harrisburg, PA: Morehouse Publishing, 2002), 77.

[16] Dr. Howard and Geraldine Taylor, *Hudson Taylor's Spiritual Secret* (Chicago: Moody, 2009), 240.

going to cost you something—and to remind you that *He is worth it!*

Please look at your schedule and preferences and ask, "Dear God, what small changes can I make today in order to allow You more sway over my life, to welcome You to do in and through me whatever You want?" Then bravely act on what He reveals.

TOPICAL REFLECTIONS

1. Describe the general approach you use to stay in fellowship with God. How might adopting the kind of start-each-day-with-Him plan that Anita presents help you?

2. Read Mark 1:35. How does the passage support the idea of holding a morning quiet time?

3. Which of the five steps for having a successful quiet time do you think would prove most helpful were you to adopt it? Explain.

4. Read Psalm 46:1–2 and 62:7–8. Explain how meeting with God daily at a set place and time might help to solidify your thoughts of Him as your Refuge.

5. Which quote or story that Anita uses in this chapter most inspires you to meet with God consistently? Why?

CHAPTER 5

REMEMBER THE REWARDS OF RELATIONSHIP-BUILDING

"You will seek me and find me when you seek me with all of your heart."
– Jeremiah 29:13

BACK IN 2005, when I first felt God calling me to put together a workshop encouraging other believers to dig into their Bibles through structured quiet times, my mind immediately began to try to talk myself out of that crazy idea! I busily listed all the reasons people would not be interested in what I had to say. (Does your brain work like that? I admit I find my own terribly noisy and discouraging sometimes.) In addition to my concerns that they wouldn't want to hear from someone without a theological PhD were worries like these: *Why would anyone give up time to attend a workshop? I'm not certain most will be able to see the need to seek God daily on their own; some will probably think I'm urging them to do a preacher's work. Few will want to devote a set amount of time to Scripture study each day; our culture likes downtime, and my ideas cut into that. Many will feel they have enough going on, as if I'm just adding to their burdens.* When I realized I was about to let such fears talk me out of the notion I knew God had placed on my heart, I went straight to Him.

"Dear Lord," I said, "I know that through the matter of Twila's file and how her reading it opened the door of relationship between us, You've given me a powerful story that can help people want to open Scripture, to get to know You better. And I thank You that You've given me this passion to encourage people to be in Your Word and to speak to You regularly. But, Father, You know that what I'll be asking people to do if I go through with this idea is not exactly easy. Many will find endless reasons to dismiss my teaching if they are willing to hear it at all. Would You please help me replace this negative list of excuses flooding my mind? Will You please give me good, motivating reasons I can share with Your people so they will be encouraged to try and hopefully stay the course of seeking You? And will You please, through the power of the Holy Spirit, allow them to see evidence of a changed life, fruit that You have produced, when they look at me—evidence that will itself draw them toward seeking You personally?"

> Whatever sincere effort I'd invested in prioritizing God had yielded incredibly rich dividends.

Now this may surprise you, but I didn't receive a divine email in response to my request for motivating reasons to share with people. There was no pretty greeting card that came in the mailbox that week, full of the kind of bullet points I was hoping for. Rather, over the next few days the Lord got me reflecting on what I'd gained during my brief time of practicing a lifestyle of seeking Him first—much as I've outlined in this book thus far. And every time I grew aware of another specific blessing, I wrote it down. What amazed me most as I reviewed the list was that I really hadn't had to do anything impressive to receive any of the wonderful gifts I'd noted. Rather, each had come as a natural consequence of simply spending consistent, dedicated time with my

Creator. Whatever sincere effort I'd invested in prioritizing God had yielded *incredibly rich* dividends.

1. In Intentionally Meeting with the Lord Daily, I'd Grown to Truly Know Him.

Skeptics sometimes cite God's "un-knowability" as a reason to reject Christianity. "Why bother acknowledging someone you can't be certain exists?" some ask. But as I've grown in my Christian walk, I've found that not only is God's existence amazingly unquestionable—He is also wonderfully knowable.

In John 17, just prior to the events that would become Easter weekend, Jesus prayed to God the Father. One thing I love about the passage is that in it Jesus noted He wasn't praying just for His twelve disciples, including Peter, James, and John. He said He was praying "also for those who [would] believe in [Him] through their message" (v. 20). That's a direct reference to every Jesus-follower, including you and me! In verse 3 He also gave insight into just how rich a gift He came to provide us. In addition to passages that clarify that eternal life means a blissful existence with God beyond the grave (John 6:40; Matthew 25:46), He said, "Now this is eternal life: that they may know you, the only true God, and Jesus Christ, whom you have sent."

Notice the verb tense. It says, "Now this is eternal life." And what is eternal life? Actually *knowing* God the Father and Jesus Christ like we know our friends and closest family members. Frankly, that just blows my mind. Yet it's true! Even the Greek here, which is the original language in which the New Testament was penned, bears it out. The Greek term translated in our English Bibles as "know" is *ginasko*. It means to know in a completed sense, to know in the sense of personal relationship.[1] God wants us to

---

[1] Spiros Zodhiates, ed., *The Complete Word Study New Testament* (Chattanooga, TN: AMG Publishers, 1994), 372.

know Him in much the same way that I came to know Paul well through our spending years living together.

Another illustration may help us envision how this could work since we don't have the benefit of seeing God in the flesh and getting to know Him in a more traditional sense. Suppose you and I bump into each other at a busy Starbucks. While waiting for our orders, we introduce ourselves and easily connect over our love for Jesus. We find out we live about thirty minutes apart; and since we are really enjoying each other's company, we decide we should get to know each other better. To eliminate travel time, we set up an appointment to connect via phone call every morning of the next month. For twenty minutes each day, we will chat before work.

By the time that month is up, we realize we have tons in common and each benefit from the friendship. Our talks become an important part of our days. So we agree that for the next eleven months we will keep having our morning conversations.

I think you'll agree that you and I could not help but know one another better through so much intentional interaction. Even without the benefit of eye contact and hugs and being able to read one another's facial expressions and body language, we'd each soon be able to say honestly, "Hey, I *know* her! She's my dearest friend." In fact, we'd be able to speak at length about one another to our other friends. Such closeness, such familiarity are natural consequences of really spending time with someone, even if physical distance interferes.

My point is that if each day you get up and say, "I just want to spend some time with You today, Jesus," and really do so, getting to know Him can't be helped!

Yet I need to bring up a very sad verse and its implications here. In Jeremiah 4:22 God had something tragic to say about His people of Old Testament times. He lamented, "My people are fools; they do not know me." My suspicion is that the Lord could easily make the same claim against many who think of themselves as His people now, in the church age. What makes me so pessimistic? Well, if you think about it, you'll note that there are many Christians who don't talk about Jesus very much. Though tasked with telling the world about Him (see 2 Corinthians 5:20), they feel awkward about even bringing Him up. The majority, I suspect, simply aren't confident they know enough about Him to do a good job of it. Worse, many are much more familiar with what the world set in opposition to Christ thinks than they are familiar with what He says. The great news is that if we believers are really spending time with Him, we can't help but gain confidence and passion. In fact, an obsession with Him tends to spill over into conversations as a result! As surely as a bride-to-be can't help but talk about her adored fiancé to anyone who'll listen, those who really know Christ can't help but speak of Him lovingly either. Dedicated time with Him is what makes all the difference.

2. In Intentionally Meeting with the Lord Daily, My Thinking Was Being Transformed.

I've admitted that I used to start my morning by taking in a big dose of bad news from the paper. I also came clean about what was once a soap opera addiction. No doubt about it: both of those seemingly harmless-at-the-time daily habits of mine influenced the way I thought.

At this point in my life (I am now in my sixties) I've come to realize that our Western culture—whether through social media, blogs and magazines, movies and television, or even advertising—is constantly seeking to shape the way you and I process things. And that can be a dangerous thing. While some of the shaping that comes from culture is benign and some is even helpful, we believers must be alert to the fact that our enemy the devil loves to influence people's thinking and has proven remarkably successful at using the tactic to undermine many biblical values once foundational to American culture—like marriage's once uncontested definition of being between one man and one woman committed to one another for life.² As surely as he once hissed to Eve, "Did God really say . . . ?" Satan is constantly urging people to adopt countless practices and ideologies that run counter to biblical teaching—to their own harm (see Genesis 3:1). Colossians 2:8 specifically warns us, "Beware lest anyone cheat you through philosophy and empty deceit, according to the tradition of men, according to the basic principles of the world and not according to Christ" (NKJV). "The whole world," 1 John 5:19 points out, "is under the control of the evil one." One consistent message in Scripture is that if we aren't careful, we will become so like the world—and the enemy—in thought that our faith will make little practical difference to how we live.

Romans 12:2 reminds us that we must not only stand guard against being influenced by the devil's tactics but also seek thought transformation. Paul said, "Do not conform to the pattern of this world, but be transformed by the renewing of your mind." We believers, he said elsewhere, are to "have the mind of Christ" (1 Corinthians 2:16). In other words, he called Christians not to take their cues from the world at all but to let Jesus and His Word transform the way we think. Spending regular, focused time with God is mission-critical to doing this successfully.

Reverend Billy Graham once wisely noted, "It seems that some diabolic mastermind is running the affairs of this world and that his chief objective is to brainwash Christians and to get them to conform to the world. The world's sewage system threatens to contaminate the stream of Christian thought."³ By regularly placing ourselves under the authority of God's Word and in focused fellowship with our Creator, you and I are well on our way to following the advice of 2 Corinthians 7:1 on this matter. There

---

² The biblical view of marriage appears first in Genesis 2:23–25 and is reinforced by Jesus in Matthew 19:4–6.

³ Billy Graham, *Unto the Hills: A Daily Devotional* (Nashville, TN: Thomas Nelson, 2010), 73.

Paul the apostle said, "Let us purify ourselves from everything that contaminates . . . , perfecting holiness out of reverence for God."

As I've chosen to get under the influence of God's Word, He has changed the way I think in so many important ways! I no longer let the world tell me how to think about moral issues, how I should respond to world affairs, or even what I should consider important in life. I take my cues from the Lord.

For instance, consider the COVID-19 pandemic that swept our country and others all over the world, and the resulting panic it created. While I followed all the protocol and grieved with those who lost loved ones during that sad time—and even endured a blessedly mild case of the virus myself—I refused to allow fear of the thing to get hold of my heart. Rather, I held on to and lived out the anti-anxiety prescription I knew from Scripture, from spending so much time getting to know the Lord and how He wants me to think:

> Do not be anxious about anything, but in every situation, by prayer and petition, with thanksgiving, present your requests to God. And the peace of God, which transcends all understanding, will guard your hearts and your minds in Christ Jesus.
>
> Finally, . . . whatever is true, whatever is noble, whatever is right, whatever is pure, whatever is lovely, whatever is admirable—if anything is excellent or praiseworthy—think about such things. (Philippians 4:6–8)

Sure enough, as long as I allowed my thinking to be transformed by what God urges me to do "in every situation," I found peace. In fact . . .

3. In Intentionally Meeting with the Lord Daily, I'd Grown Far More Peaceful.

Back when my Christian life boiled down to me listening to sermons and trying to apply them now and then, as if the whole of my spiritual walk was up to me to figure out based on whatever I could glean from my pastor, I often felt defeated, as if I could never measure up, as if everything in my life were working against the effort and that truly living for Jesus was hopeless. Job 3:26 says, "I have no peace, no quietness; I have no rest, but only turmoil." We can easily feel that way if we're trying to live for the Lord without letting Him help us. And when we refuse to spend time with Him and just try to power through on our own, that's exactly what we're doing! Second Peter 1:3 says, "[God's] divine power has given us everything we need for a godly life through our knowledge of him who called us by his own glory and goodness." As I grow in personal knowledge of Him, I've found I grow in reliance on His divine power. And I stop trying to make the Christian life about me and my efforts, and instead live for Him and His glory!

It was this change in thinking that helped me begin to appropriate and experience certain biblical promises. Psalm 119:165 says, "Great peace have those who love [God's] law, and nothing can make them stumble." Isaiah 26:3 says, "[God] will keep in perfect peace those whose minds are steadfast, because they trust in [Him]." As we believe and confess these promises with our mouths, we come to understand why Jesus is called the "Prince of Peace" (see Isaiah 9:6).

On a side note, one day as I was reflecting on exactly what it means that Jesus is the Prince of Peace, I grabbed my Hebrew dictionary and saw that one of the definitions for *prince* is "chief" or "greatest."[4] A smile came to my face as I pictured Him as my Chief of Peace!

---

[4] Robert L. Thomas, ThD, *New American Standard Exhaustive Concordance of the Bible: Hebrew-Aramaic and Greek Dictionaries,* s.v. "prince" (Nashville, TN: Holman Bible Publishers, 1981), 1611.

4. In Intentionally Meeting with the Lord Daily, I Had Not Only Come to Better Understand His Will but Had Also Grown Quicker to Do It.

As surely as Scripture is loaded with encouraging verses for Christians, it has a few strong warnings too. One that used to scare me was Matthew 7:21. There Jesus said, "Not everyone who says to me, 'Lord, Lord,' will enter the kingdom of heaven, but only the one who does the will of my Father." This passage bothered me because I knew there were many times when I ignored what Scripture reveals about God's will, and I had no doubt that there were plenty of things He willed that I was completely ignorant about. Having a dismissive attitude about what God wants may, Jesus warns us, mean we're not truly saved!

Thankfully, my problem of not following God's will out of ignorance quickly began to take care of itself as I grew more familiar with the Bible personally. Not only did I get a better understanding of its *do*s and *don't*s, but I developed a grasp of God's character and what He wants of His people that helped me make wiser decisions and avoid getting tangled in sin as often.

Yet even with that growing knowledge, I still struggled in the obedience department. After all, sin often offers immediate gratification; the blessings of obeying can be a lot slower in coming!

Many years ago, for instance, when our first daughter was getting married, we went to the bridal shop. As Shelly was being outfitted in potential gowns for her big day, the saleslady zeroed in on me. She told me she had the perfect mother-of-the-bride dress for my build and coloring. And what she hurried off to fetch turned out to be one of the most beautiful dresses I'd ever seen; instantly I loved it. The strategically placed rhinestones down its front winked at me under the shop's bright lighting, practically begging me to take it home. But then I saw the price tag. That thing cost almost as much as the gown Shelly had finally settled on! I knew I couldn't ask my hard-working husband to take on that outrageous extra expense, so I graciously declined it and said I wanted to keep looking. Weeks later, however, as time was running out and I had yet to find another dress I loved, I handed that same saleslady our credit card and took that sparkling garment to my own closet.

My conscience nagged as soon as I left the store. I even prayed a selfish prayer that God would keep Paul from finding out about my splurge—which by the way, is the kind of prayer the Lord ignores (see James 4:3). Unsurprisingly, before the sun had even set on the day, Paul asked me what the dress had cost. And though I knew it is God's will that I "put off falsehood," I dodged the question as long as possible, trying to come up with a palatable lie about the garment's price (see Ephesians 4:25). Though my husband is wonderfully even-tempered, I was just sure he'd kill me if he knew how much of his hard-earned money I'd blown on a dress destined to be worn one time!

In the end, I did come clean about the dress, and—as you've no doubt guessed—my dear husband did not demand my life as payment for the selfish indulgence. Rather, he let it be my birthday and Christmas gift that year. But the inner turmoil over this matter that I've described testifies to how very easy (and sadly, even comfortable!) it used to be for me to tell little half-truths and to make excuses for why it was okay for me to sin (that is, miss the mark) in certain instances—even as I was spending dedicated morning times with the Lord.

After many months of prioritizing my relationship with God, however, I did slowly begin to lose interest in such tactics. As I grew closer with Jesus, I eventually stopped wondering how much leash He'd allow me if I just ignored His will to suit my selfishness. Instead, I found myself increasingly determined to please Him, more trusting that what He wanted of me was best despite the consequences. Amazingly, I continue to find that the more I seek to know Him personally, the more He gives me the desire to want to do His will. In fact, these days I'm usually quick to do it.

I'D LIKE TO offer a helpful side note on this matter. Many believers hear talk of doing God's will and immediately leap to wondering what His will is in terms of who they should marry, what job they should take, or whether they should move from this city to that one—as if God can be pleased with a person only should she make the right menu selections.

But what I've discovered through God's Word is that He works through the wise decisions His people make—like Joseph's choice to have the Egyptians store their grain in preparation for the coming famine (Genesis 41:34–36)—as well as through the foolish ones, like Jacob's agreement to take four wives instead of one (Genesis 28–30:26). In that case, the Lord generously accepted the children of all four wives as the twelve patriarchs of the nation of Israel—though to say Jacob endured a lot of family drama for his lack of wisdom is an understatement.

> As I grew closer with Jesus, I eventually stopped wondering how much leash He'd allow me if I just ignored His will to suit my selfishness.

When you think about God's will, don't immediately focus on His will on a certain big question. Rather, practice thinking about His revealed will—what you can specifically know He wants for your life because of what He's told you in the Bible—and doing it. It is, for instance, His will that none should perish but that all should have eternal life through trusting in Jesus as Lord (see 2 Peter 3:9). So in placing faith in Jesus, you've made a choice to live in His will! Moreover, you can rest assured that it's God's will for you to share the good news about Jesus with others. Also, it is His will that people live in holiness and bear good fruit, finding out what pleases Him and doing it—even if that's as simple as giving money to help the poor or being kind to children. So each time you make even a tiny choice along those lines, you are choosing to live in His will. Moreover, it is His will that we love Him above all things and that we aim to love others as ourselves (see Matthew 22:36–39). So as you honor God and love people—even difficult people—you are doing God's will.

Life's big questions like "Whom should I marry?" are also helped when we learn to think this way. For instance, if you are single and living in light of God's revealed will on the matter of dating only believers (see 2 Corinthians 6:14) and desire that your spouse help you bring up any children you might have in the fear and knowledge of the Lord (see Ephesians 6:4), you'll be equipped to make a godly decision on that matter.

The better we get to know the Lord through spending time in His Word, the more readily we will live in light of His will, in matters big and small. It's a natural consequence of doing so.

5. In Intentionally Meeting with the Lord Daily, I'd Realized My Spiritual Gifting and Found Myself Equipped to Use It.

It was in reading 1 Corinthians during my quiet time that I realized I had a spiritual gift that the Holy Spirit had picked out just for me: "To each one the manifestation of the Spirit is given for the common good. . . . [H]e distributes them to each one, just as he determines" (1 Corinthians 12:7, 11). Curious, I used my concordance to see what else the Bible says about the topic and noted that spiritual gifts include prophesying, serving, teaching, encouraging, giving, leadership, mercy, knowledge, faith, healing, discernment, and speaking in tongues.

Prior to that, I thought people were able to serve God only through their talents. For instance, my mother is a great musician. She used her talent for playing the piano, organ, and harp in helping to lead musical worship at our church. And Dad has a talent for public speaking, making pastoring a good fit for him.

True, God can certainly work through a person's talents and skill sets to bring glory to Himself. But it's wrong to assume that the only people who can really be used of God are those who have abilities that can be showcased in a typical church service. Back when I thought like that, part of me feared that if I were to truly surrender my life to God, I might have to find and develop a church-service-useful talent like playing the organ—a thought I just hated. (My poor mom tried to teach me piano when I was in my preteen years, but I was somewhat rebellious during lessons and she'd have to pause mid-session to pray over my terrible attitude!)

Spending time with the Lord in His Word eventually helped me to replace my old "I've gotta have a certain kind of talent if I am to serve the Lord" thinking with the sense of wonder and excitement that comes in knowing that every Christian has been given a gift meant to be used to glorify Him. Each has at least one spiritual tool that can be easily employed as a natural extension of how we were created and of who we are in Him.

My spiritual gift, for example, is encouraging. I love to lift other believers up with kind words and through pointing them to appropriate and edifying passages of Scripture. I find great joy and fulfillment in doing so. It's like it's down in my wiring.

Come to think of it, as surely as I hated practicing piano as a teenager, I loved practicing to be a part of my high school cheerleading squad! Cheering my school's team on to victory and trying to get the people up in the stands to really engage in the game came naturally for me. I was never intimidated by the large crowds. The more the better! I wanted to get everyone fired up to encourage our football and basketball teams to victory! And that is exactly how I am today, passionately rooting for my believing teammates in their walks with the Lord and urging them to be more than passive observers of God's work in the world. Though I had to really work at the physical aspects of cheerleading (I can't say I have any real gymnastic talent), I don't even have to think about building up my family of faith through words. God has put a deep, natural desire in my heart to inspire the church to seek Him first! Acting on that has brought me such tremendous joy that it makes my heart dance.

First Peter 4:10 says, "Each of you [believers] should use whatever gift you have received to serve others, as faithful stewards of God's grace." That makes it certain that our heavenly Father has equipped you with a spiritual gift and wants you to use it to build His kingdom too! Once you identify it and start using it, you'll find a sense of purposefulness that most people can only dream about.

Never forget, though, that God wants to use the spiritual gifts and also the talents He has given His people for the specific goal of building up the body of Christ. He never gives us gifts to serve ourselves, but to serve others.

Moreover, as you serve, remember that God's Word is to be the manual behind everything you do and say. In 2 Timothy 3:16–17 the apostle Paul said, "All Scripture is God-breathed and is useful for teaching, rebuking, correcting and training in righteousness, so that the servant of God may be thoroughly equipped for every good work." Such works, Ephesians 2:10 reminds us, were actually "prepared in advance for us to do." It's in knowing God through the study of Scripture and in spending time with Him that we are prepared to look for and obediently do whatever He wants.

6. In Intentionally Meeting with the Lord Daily, I'd Become a True Worshiper.

In the New Testament account of Jesus's meeting with a Samaritan woman, Jesus responded to her question about worshiping God. He said, "A time is coming and has now come when the true worshipers will worship the Father in the Spirit and in truth, for they are the kind of worshipers the Father seeks" (John 4:23). Indeed, God is looking for people who will worship Him wholeheartedly out of an understanding of the truth of who He is. I've found that in starting my day with God and His written Word, I not only know what is true about Him but also am stirred to worship.

True, worshiping can involve singing His praises, but it's actually much more than that. As Oswald Chambers explained, "Worship is giving the best we have unreservedly to God."[5] And in Colossians 3:17 the apostle Paul said it this way: "[W]hatever you do, whether in word or deed, do it all in the name of the Lord Jesus, giving thanks to God the Father through him." Every act of obedience to God and in service to others, then, is worship! And even simply giving thanks to God is a way to worship Him. In short, worship involves telling God thank You and living in such a way as to express the same.

7. In Intentionally Meeting with the Lord Daily, I'd Become a Joyful Person.

Many mornings I wake up re-experiencing a hurt or sorrow that came knocking the day before, which leads to me feeling depressed; nevertheless, I head to my chair to meet with God. As I pray and pick up my Bible despite what my feelings are telling me, I always find my burdens feel significantly lighter as a result. No doubt this is due in part to the fact that in going to Him with my troubles, I'm allowing the Lord to help bear my burdens (see Psalm 68:19). But another part of it comes down to the reality that rings so beautifully through these quotes:

Minister William Vander Hoven said, "Joy is not the absence of trouble but the presence of Christ."[6] "In your presence," King

---

[5] Oswald Chambers, *My Utmost Devotional Bible* (Nashville, TN: Thomas Nelson, 1997), 413.

[6] William Vander Hoven, *Pentecostal Evangel* (Springfield, MO: General Council of the Assemblies of God, 2000), 26.

David said to God, "You will fill me with joy" (Psalm 16:11). Psalm 28:7 says, "The Lord is my strength and my shield; my heart trusts in him, and he helps me. My heart leaps for joy." And author Oswald Chambers said, with a nod to the fact that the only true joy is based on a personal relationship to God, "[I]f I am full of the joy of the Lord, it will pour out of every cell."[7]

One of my favorite joy quotes is in John 15:11. Jesus said, "I have told you this so that my joy may be in you and that your joy may be complete." That insight is directly linked to the discussion leading up to it. In verses 1–10 Jesus told His followers to remain in Him, to remain in His words (that is, Scripture), and to remain in His love. When we do, it seems we really can hold onto joy in spite of even terrible situations.

Because it's my favorite word, as well as central to my workshop ministry known as JoyShop, I've long had *joy* plastered all over my house. It's a subtle way to plant the seed of joy in myself and others. That being said, I recall a time when I was at the bank with my son Josh, who was setting up online banking. The teller asked Josh for the answers to several security questions and one of them was this: "What is your mother's middle name?" Josh immediately replied, "Joy!" Though my middle name is Kay, I understood he'd drawn that wrong conclusion from seeing the word prominently featured all over our home. I had to laugh even as I corrected him. Now the memory makes me think about how wonderful it would be if every believer lived with such an undercurrent of joy—despite all circumstances—that people just associated the concept with them.

---

[7] Chambers, *My Utmost Devotional Bible*, 1230.

8. In Intentionally Meeting with the Lord Daily, I'd Found Myself Blessed and Starting to Live so as to Bless Others.

When God called Abram, patriarch of Israel, He pronounced these words: "I will make you into a great nation, and I will bless you; I will make your name great, and you will be a blessing" (Genesis 12:2).[8]

Notice that in the first part of the passage, God told His man Abram that he would personally be blessed. While this does not guarantee that all who trust in the Lord will never face difficulty or that we will all be healthy and prosperous or even "great"—that is, famous in the sense that Abraham is—the principle of generally living under God's blessing is one appearing throughout Scripture. For instance, Psalm 112:1 says, "Blessed are those who fear the Lord, who find great delight in his commands." In the New Testament Luke 11:28 says, "Blessed . . . are those who hear the word of God and obey it." Sixty-plus years of life have taught me that there are wonderful blessings in knowing who I am in God and in functioning out of who I know Him to be!

Now, in the second part of Genesis 12:2 Abram was told that he "[would] be a blessing," too. And this is every bit as exciting as the personal benefits that come with following the Lord. One dictionary defines *blessing* as "a gift of God."[9] Just think about that! In Christ, and through spending time with Him, we prepare to serve others in such a way that they will feel they have received a gift of God through us.

This matter of being a blessing isn't necessarily linked to doing something big for others, like gifting them with a mortgage payment to help them navigate a hard season or counseling them through a challenging time, or even doing something like teaching

---

[8] Abram is better known as "Abraham."

[9] *The Oxford American Desk Dictionary: Major New Edition*, s.v. "blessing" (Oxford, UK: Oxford University Press, 1998), 60.

a Sunday school class. (Though, of course, it can be.) Often, I think, God's people are seen by others as blessings simply as they go about doing life and loving Jesus to the best of their ability.

What happened years ago when Paul and I visited a tiny church while vacationing in West Virginia illustrates this beautifully. That Sunday morning, after we settled into our seats among those forty or so worshipers, I saw an elderly gentleman slowly shuffling his way toward our pew. He sat down at its end, looking winded yet somehow satisfied. Two things held my attention as I wondered about the expression on his face. First, he was hooked up to an oxygen tank; every inhale he made sounded loud and labored and caused his apparatus to make an odd clicking sound. Second, the man had balanced his worn, open Bible on his knee and kept running his hand over it gently.

As I stood with everyone else but him to sing, I quickly noticed that the man's breathing—not to mention his oxygen machine—could be heard over the music. After the first song closed and the next one began, the Lord revealed to my heart that the fellow I was tempted to find annoying was so in love with Him that he'd come to church when he could barely breathe. Though most who suffered a simple sniffle would use it as an excuse to stay home from church, that man had gone to great lengths to come to hear the Word preached and to be near other worshipers. Thus, that elderly fellow, through his dedication, was an example to the rest of us. In simply showing up, he'd become a blessing to me. Years later, in fact, I still fall a little more in love with the Lord when I think of him.

Simply in being faithful to love God, we too are in position to bless others. The closer we draw to Him, in fact, the more likely we are to think of and act on ways that point others to Him—and like the man I've mentioned, to do so even when we aren't thinking about it, even if no one ever tells us (this side of Heaven) that we did.

AS I LOOKED over this list, and it is just a partial list, of the many blessings I have come to experience as a direct result of spending time with Jesus daily, I asked myself, "Who wouldn't want these blessings in their life?" I saw for myself that in intentionally meeting with the Lord every day, I'd grown to truly know Him, that my thinking was being transformed, and that I'd grown far more peaceful. Not only had I come to better understand God's will, but also I'd grown quicker to do it. I'd realized my spiritual gifting and found myself equipped to use it. I'd become a true worshiper. And I'd found myself not just blessed but choosing to live in such a way so as to bless others. In other words, I'd started to truly experience the abundant life in Christ for which I'd so longed.

Will you please pause and pray through the above paragraph, asking God to help you seek Him faithfully and so experience these amazing rewards too? "Anyone who will take the time to enter into an intimate relationship with God," discipleship author Henry Blackaby encourages us, really "can see God do extraordinary things."[10]

---

[10] Henry T. Blackaby and Claude V. King, *Experiencing God: Knowing and Doing the Will of God* (Nashville: Broadman and Holman, 2004), 45.

TOPICAL REFLECTIONS

1. Read James 4:8a and 10. How do Anita's eight main points in this chapter support this truth?

2. Give an example of how you've seen this statement prove true: "As surely as a bride-to-be can't help but talk about her adored fiancé to anyone who'll listen, those who really know Christ can't help but speak of Him." (Bonus points if you can also name a New Testament character who illustrates this point.)

3. What does it look like to "have the mind of Christ"? Could this be said of you? Defend your answer.

4. Review the spiritual gifts listed on page 92. Which of them do you suspect the Lord has given you as a tool for serving the church, the body of Christ? Hint: often our spiritual gifts are discovered in the things we just naturally love to do.

5. Which of the natural consequences of intentionally meeting with the Lord daily is most appealing to you? Why?

CHAPTER 6

BEWARE OF COMMON ENEMY TACTICS

*"If you don't have time for prayer and Bible study,
Satan is winning the war."*
– Anonymous

AS I REFLECTED on the long list of blessings I had begun to experience as a natural result of seeking daily audience with Jesus, I had to ask myself why it took me so long to grasp the teaching of Matthew 6:33 when I had known this verse by heart for many years! So many decades had been wasted and many blessings had been missed, simply because I hadn't prioritized welcoming the Lord into my days! The more I considered my own laziness on that point, the more I grieved over what a tragic waste that was. I'd heard of the importance of pursuing closeness with God, yet in reality I hadn't actively pursued Him.

Today I recognize it's usually counterproductive to mourn the past. We must always press forward spiritually, "forgetting what is behind and straining toward what is ahead" (Philippians 3:13). But a few helpful realizations did eventually rise out of my frustration with my own spiritual procrastination.

First came this idea. A believer's journey with Christ is like a race down a long path. It starts at the moment of salvation and continues on until the moment of death, the minute when faith becomes sight. Ideally, we grow ever more committed in our relationship with Jesus all the way, thus running down the whole path. Yet—and this is my second realization—as surely as most of us battle some apathy along the way, we will all sometimes be confronted by what I call *road hazards*, strategically placed enemy tactics designed to slow our spiritual progress or make it grind to a halt. If we aren't fully committed to reaching the finish line of life to hear Jesus say, "Well done, good and faithful servant," we'll easily allow such road hazards to succeed against us (see Matthew 25:21), maybe even to make us forget we're in a race at all.

In this chapter I'll identify some of the most common road hazards I have encountered, tools our enemy, Satan, places in and along our paths to discourage us from living with dedicated focus on God. The name "Satan" means "adversary" or "opposer."[1] He first shows up in the biblical narrative in Genesis 3; there he appears as the serpent who tempts Eve (see Revelation 12:9). Bible scholars believe that Ezekiel 28:12–17, though poetically addressing a human king, also alludes to Satan's early history; Jesus seems to support this by saying, "I saw Satan fall like lightning from heaven" (Luke 10:18). Regardless, in John 10:10 Jesus speaks of him as a "thief [that] comes only to steal and kill and destroy."

Since you initially repented and received Jesus as your Lord and Savior, you've been sealed with the Holy Spirit (see Ephesians 4:30). That means you cannot be snatched out of God's hand; you are His for all eternity (see John 10:27–29; Romans 8:38–39). So here's what the devil—who really hates that—does. He focuses his efforts on robbing you of the riches that are yours in Christ. He will set up hazard after hazard, often disguised in common, everyday

---

[1] Spiros Zodhiates, ed., *The Complete Word Study New Testament* (Chattanooga, TN: AMG Publishers, 1994), 1282.

occurrences, each specifically designed to keep you from grasping or living in light of your true identity as a child of God. The devil will work to defeat you with doubts, lure you off pace with endless petty distractions, and capture you in potholes of busyness and fear. He'll also try to draw you into a thorny bramble called "worldliness." Satan is so good at all this that the Bible warns believers that he "prowls around like a roaring lion looking for someone to devour" (1 Peter 5:8). To put that concept into the imagery I'll use throughout this chapter, imagine him as Wile E. Coyote in the old Looney Tunes cartoons. If we Christians are roadrunners darting down the path of life in Jesus, Satan is the coyote who's always working hard to make us stumble into a trap, pause for a deadly snack, or veer off to our own detriment. But unlike the coyote, he's often tragically successful.

The great news is that in diligently spending regular, focused time with God through repentance, Bible reading, and prayer, we're well on our way to steering clear of a lot of road hazards due to personal disinterest in them. But because the enemy likes to use the same basic tactics against us repeatedly at various points along our journeys, I want to make sure you can recognize the five most common.

1. Doubt

One hazard that's often effective against God's people is doubt—and it may as well be a spike strip. Doubt is best understood in light of its end goal: unbelief. No, I'm not talking about the kind of unbelief that makes unsaved people deny Jesus as Lord. Rather, I'm talking about what happens when we believers entertain doubts that arise, allowing them to stab and hinder to the point that we either fail to start seeking God past salvation or eventually stop seeking the Lord as we once did. This, in fact, was the first way the thief tried to rob me of enjoying life in Christ. As surely as God speaks His truths through Scripture, Satan will speak his lies through doubts, causing us to distrust God and question His love, goodness, and kindness toward us.

If you think back to what I shared near the start of this book, you might remember there was a brief season in which I didn't believe that God—my heavenly Father—was to be trusted on every point. For instance, He said in His Word, "Obey your parents in everything" (Colossians 3:20). But I felt it made more sense to honor them in most things and sneak behind their backs in others. Later I felt that God should not be bothered with bailing me out of the mess I'd made in getting pregnant as a teen. Acting on that lie was in direct disregard of what His Word says in Psalm 50:15, that we are to "call on [the Lord] in the day of trouble," and Hebrews 4:16, which says, "Let us come boldly to the throne of our gracious God. There we will receive his mercy, and we will find grace to help us when we need it most" (NLT). Further, for a minute there, I didn't believe He was able to bring any good out of the sinful choices I'd made. Just as the devil wanted, I bought the lie that I couldn't possibly have a good future left! Yet doing so ignored what the Bible says in Romans 8:28, that "all things work together for good to those who love God" (NKJV), and in Jeremiah 29:11, that "[God knows] the plans [He has] for [us], ... plans to give [us] hope and a future." I was very aware of both of those famous verses in particular, even then.

As I embraced wrong thinking, even what I'd thought I understood of the Bible was of no value to me because I did not combine it with faith (see Hebrews 4:2). And that is exactly what the enemy aims to accomplish when he sets a road hazard of doubt. "Satan's greatest victories," one Christian author insisted, "do not lie in getting unbelievers to heap vice upon vice, but in lulling believers into taking God's Word lightly,"[2] into making us distrustful of it—especially when we need it most!

---

[2] Thomas C. Peters, *Cherish the Word: Reflections on Luther's Spirituality* (St. Louis: Christian Publishing House, 2000), 62.

In fact, the devil *loves* to make us doubt God and what He says. So when spikes of doubt arise, we must dodge them by keeping a firm hold on God's Word being the changeless, trustworthy source it is. We must not entertain any thought to the contrary. As pastor D. L. Moody warned, "Unbelief is the mother of all sins!"[3] Look no further than Genesis 3 to see how Adam and Eve's simple choice to disbelieve what God said on one point opened the gate to countless other sins as well as ushering in endless sorrow and suffering.

As I thought about this doubt topic, the Lord brought a particular Scripture passage to mind. In it he explained to Moses's successor, Joshua, how to have a prosperous and successful life. God said this of Scripture: "Keep this . . . always on your lips; meditate on it day and night, so that you may be careful to do everything written in it. Then you will be prosperous and successful" (Joshua 1:8). At this point in my journey with Jesus, I can testify that it really is in taking God at His Word and tenaciously living by it that we successfully avoid enemy road hazards—especially this one called doubt—and instead prosper spiritually, mentally, and emotionally.

> It really is in taking God at His Word and tenaciously living by it that we avoid enemy road hazards—especially this one called doubt—and instead prosper spiritually, mentally, and emotionally.

One unexpected situation in my life that seemed impossible at the time serves as a good illustration here. During my fifth pregnancy, people began making comments like these: "Wow, Anita! That baby seems to be growing really fast!" and "Are you sure you're not having twins? You're awful big for your due date!" Since I knew from experience that each baby tends to stretch a girl's belly out a

---

[3] Dwight L. Moody, *Secret Power* (Newberry, FL: Bridge-Logos Foundation, 2006), 97.

little more quickly because her abdominal muscles have been loosened, I dismissed that "twins" word that kept coming up and tried not to be bothered by all the insinuations I was getting fat. Besides, I just *knew* a kind God would never ask me to handle two babies at one time, especially since I already had a seven-year-old daughter and her four-year-old sister to keep up with back then. (And since my husband was often putting in eighty-hour work weeks at the time!) Nevertheless, wouldn't you know it? In my sixth month the doctor told me that twins were indeed on their way. And, oh, did doubts about whether I'd ever survive come calling! The only thing that got me through it was repeating *and believing* one amazing promise in Scripture. Philippians 4:13 says, "I can do all things through Christ who strengthens me" (NKJV). If He would truly strengthen me through the coming adventure, I reasoned, then God really was kind—even if there was a panicked minute there when the thought of twins seemed like a mean joke.

Thankfully, I can report that all throughout delivery, potty training, and everything else that comes with raising twin boys for eighteen years, I chose to keep believing that I could mother those two as well as my daughters because Jesus would give me strength. The Bible said so! As a result, in spite of all my initial doubt about my ability and even God's wisdom in sending me multiples, I've now *seen* the Lord deliver on His Word. And I now have the pleasure of watching my sons strive to live as men in love with Jesus!

2. Distraction

Another common type of road hazard the enemy likes to use against the forward progress of our journeys with God is distraction. This one works like a lure, something seemingly benign that takes our thoughts off the mission and to the nearest off-ramp. Most of the time it shows up just as you sit down to spend time with the Lord.

Maybe the phone rings. Maybe a Facebook message comes in. Maybe a sudden case of the sniffles sends you running for tissues.

Maybe your sciatica is acting up and you just can't sit in your usual quiet-time spot comfortably. Or maybe it's just a stray thought that pops into your head as you open your Bible: *I need to make sure to stop by the store and turn in that report this afternoon* or *I'm still feeling hurt this morning about what So-and-So said last night.* In all such cases, whatever tempts your mind off the task of spending time with the Lord can easily become something that leads you to go at it with less focus and enthusiasm or perhaps to forget about it altogether.

One silly—but very persistent—distraction I deal with at my home in Lancaster County, Pennsylvania, a place surrounded by beautiful farmland, is flies. I *hate* flies! And so often when I sit down to have my quiet time, a fly will show up and start buzzing all around me—even in the middle of winter when all such pests should be dead or at least hibernating! Many times, rather than ignoring their buzzing, I'll pause what I'm doing to chase them with a swatter I keep by my chair. And before I know it, I've allowed insects to rob me of five of the precious minutes I could've been spending with Jesus.

As I considered that, I looked up the word *distract* in the dictionary. It means "draw away the attention of (a person, the mind, etc.)"[4]—just like a fish jerked out of the water because it tasted the fisherman's wiggling lure! This is a strong reminder that we need to remain diligent not to allow anything—certainly not minor distractions—to hinder or reduce our scheduled time of intimacy with Jesus. Even a little procrastination can quickly lead to a lot. In our current culture of technology, I am going to venture to say that our greatest form of distraction fits in the palms of our hands—our smartphones! I have learned that I cannot even have that small piece of technology in the same room where I am meeting Jesus! It's just too tempting to pick it up and check for texts and emails,

---

[4] *The Oxford American Desk Dictionary: Major New Edition*, s.v. "distract" (Oxford, UK: Oxford University Press, 1998), 167.

which of course leads to checking social media . . . and on and on I go.

Perhaps the best advice for how to handle inevitable distractions comes from the book of Nehemiah. This man, governor of Judah, was in charge of rebuilding the crumbly wall of protection that was around Jerusalem. Several area bad guys were heartily opposed to Jerusalem having any such defenses. When they—with all the persistence of those irritating flies—attempted to distract Nehemiah from his construction efforts, he remained working at his post and simply sent them this message: "I am doing a great work, so that I cannot come down" (Nehemiah 6:3 NKJV).

Spending quality time in seeking God is also "great work," work that we as His children are to do, work that builds a spiritual wall of defense around our hearts and minds even while arming us for what's ahead (see Ephesians 6:17). We should not allow anything to keep us from giving it full attention.

3. Busyness

The third type of road hazard the enemy likes to employ against our spiritual progress is called busyness, a spiritual speed bump if ever there was one. Whereas distraction attempts to pull us away from spending time with God even as we sincerely try to do so, busyness keeps us from even getting to that point in a particular day.

An account in the Bible reveals that this particular hazard has been in use against God's people for a long time. Luke 10 speaks of an instance in which Jesus was invited over to the home of Lazarus and his sisters Mary and Martha. (Just imagine having the King of kings and Savior of the world show up to teach in your house!) Yet poor hostess Martha was so busy trying to be hospitable, likely serving up finger foods and offering drink refills, that she failed to hear what He was saying. Instead, she eventually said to the Lord—and I hope she managed to do this privately, though I doubt it—"Don't you care that my sister has left me to do the work by myself? Tell her to help me!" (v. 40). What a surprise she must've had when He replied, "Martha, Martha, . . . you are worried and upset about many things, but few are needed—or indeed only one. Mary has chosen what is better, and it will not be taken away" (vv. 41–42). Mary, by the way, had spent the afternoon sitting at Jesus's feet, soaking in every lesson He taught (v. 39)!

Nothing, nothing is better—nothing is more important—than spending time with the Lord.

Yet who among us can't relate to Martha? Most every day when I wake up, I'm confronted with a huge mental list of all the things I'd like to accomplish before the sun goes down. And I am tempted to fall for the lie that I need to get it all done before I sit down with Jesus and spend time in His Word. I do my best to say no to the lie, but I wouldn't be honest if I said I never caved in to it! Busyness can just draw me right in because I love to be efficient with my days!

When it does happen, it usually unfolds something like this. I'm headed to the living room with eight minutes to spare before my scheduled slot to meet with the Lord. I think, *Hey, I should check and see if that email I'm waiting for has come in.* So I head to my desktop hurriedly and scan the senders and subject lines. Sure enough: the email I want has arrived. But with it came two questions. So I sit and type out some simple responses. Then I read back over everything to check my grammar and to make sure I responded clearly enough. That's when I remember that the sender recently asked me to text our friend a full Bible passage she'd heard me quote in one of my workshops that she was just sure would be a real blessing to the friend, though she herself couldn't recall the whole of it or even where it was. I don't want to forget to do it again, so I take care of that too with a quick text. By that point, I'm fully awake and feeling productive. I look at the time and see I still have a minute before I'm supposed to be in my prayer chair, so

I head that way. That's when the friend to whom I texted the verse sends this reply: "Anita, that was just what I needed to hear today! Listen—I'm really struggling over something I'm dealing with at work. Could you please give me a quick call?"

Being productive and efficient by the world's standards, or even being productive in terms of serving others, can easily sidetrack us right out of prioritizing our times with God. That's why we need to see the busyness in our lives as the enemy-laid hazard it is. The apostle Paul saw it in the lives of the Corinthian believers, so he cautioned them, "I am afraid . . . your minds may somehow be led astray from your sincere and pure devotion to Christ" (2 Corinthians 11:3). In our culture it's sometimes our obsession with relentlessly checking tasks off our to-do lists that's most effective at doing so.

Busyness is a road hazard that my personality type will always have to struggle with, because I just like to get things done and I feel good when I do! But here's something I've learned over my years of dodging it regarding quiet time. In the (thankfully rare) event that I let busyness keep me out of my chair on Monday, I refuse to beat myself up about it. I confess the matter to God and make sure I'm right back on schedule with Him come Tuesday.

4. Fear

The next road hazard of which we need to be wary is fear; it's like a slippery slope leading straight into a major pothole. Our thoughts reveal whether we are about to take a big slide away from staying on course like we should. For instance, we might think . . .

- *I'm afraid God is mad at me since I missed quiet time the last two days.*
- *I feel so dense! I'm not really understanding this particular book in God's Word, so maybe reading it is just a wasted effort.*
- *My heart is so angry right now! I'm not sure God would want*

- *to speak to me while I'm feeling this way.*
- *Ugh! I've never been good at studying! The going sure is slow in my quiet times.*
- *I totally fell apart on my family last night. Won't I look like a hypocrite if they see me sitting with my open Bible today?*

If we give any of these thoughts attention as quiet time approaches, they will dump us right into a crater! Author Georgia Tanner puts it this way: "Fear is powerful and debilitating. It robs us of moving forward [or even] moving. . . . It robs us of success."[5] Indeed that is so true! When I become fearful, I just freeze up. Fear makes me think I shouldn't even try. Instead, I just cower.

For instance, after years of sharing my story and ideas publicly in workshop form, I began to give serious thought to the notion of turning my passion for Bible study into a book that could benefit small groups, mainly because people kept asking me to put my teachings into written format for group study. Yet every time I pondered it for very long, fear would keep me from looking into what it would take to make that happen. How could I—a college dropout, and a busy mother and grandmother just trying to keep her head above water—have the time or energy to write what I suspected would be a fairly complicated volume to put together? Could it even be done? Besides, I was just sure that if I did write it, no one would want to publish it, much less read it.

Time slipped by—a lot of time. But a day came when God firmly nudged my heart on the matter and even gave me a clear sign that it was time to start gathering information on how to proceed. For six weeks, though, I still continued to sit in a pothole of fear. Then I was confronted with this statement from one of the Bible teachers I listen to: "Follow God, not your fears."[6] That's

---

[5] Georgia Tanner, *Genesis: Small Stories of a Big God* (Franklin, TN: Carpenter's Son Publishing, 2019), 153.

[6] I recall that Beth Moore said this but am uncertain whether she was citing it or it was her own.

when I realized on a deeply personal level that fear is the opposite of faith and asked the Lord to see me through the production of this book, one baby step—one act of trust in Him—at a time. With His help, I climbed out of the hole and got to work. (And as chapter 6 undergoes development, I'm still trusting the outcome of this effort to Him.)

Second Timothy 1:7 says, "God has not given us a spirit of fear and timidity, but of power, love, and self-discipline" (NLT). Moreover, in the Bible we are commanded 365 times not to fear. That is one loving "Do not fear" command per day.[7] God knew that His people would struggle with fear; thus, He commands us over and over not to let it get us down.

You and I must make a choice when fears appear in our minds. We can let them have their way, which results in paralysis on par with falling into a deep hole we'll struggle to climb out of, or we can just keep moving forward in faith instead, choosing to see what comes of actively exercising trust in God. What wonderful things He can teach us and do through us when we do the latter!

5. The Pull of the Flesh (or Worldliness)
Explaining this last road hazard to our faithfully pursuing God is a little tricky. But the more I thought about it, the more I realized that this one works like thorny brambles hugging the roadsides of our Jesus journeys (you know—the nasty kind of thorn bushes that seem to reach out and snag you when you least expect it). This type of enemy tactic is particularly dangerous in that we often don't notice how close we've drifted toward it until it's too late. Rather, we just feel a poke of consequential pain brought on ourselves through a choice to sin. And if we don't immediately go to the Lord and seek His help at that first warning thorn prick, we'll

---

[7] Bill Gaultiere, "'Fear Not!' 365 Days a Year." Published March 12, 2020. *Soul Shepherding*: https://www.soulshepherding.org/fear-not-365-days-a-year/ (April 20, 2021).

often just wander further off the path and into the briar patch with disastrous results.

An example of this appears in 1 Timothy 6:10, which says, "Some people, eager for money, have wandered from the faith and pierced themselves with many griefs."

The Bible also speaks of this problem I'm describing using a different image. It talks about our "war" with the "sinful nature" (see 1 Peter 2:11; Romans 7:17–20). Both word pictures refer to the Christian's ongoing desire to indulge worldliness, to choose to sin even while trying to move forward with God.

In Galatians 5:17 the apostle Paul broke this complex matter down. He said, "The flesh desires what is contrary to the Spirit, and the Spirit what is contrary to the flesh. They are in conflict with each other." So in the context of our diligently showing up and remaining focused on God throughout our quiet times, the pull of the flesh or old sin nature is what urges us to lazily go back to bed, to worry about things that will happen later in the day, or to dismiss something the Bible says because it doesn't match up with the way we want to live. Inevitably, giving in to it leads to painful consequences that can hinder spiritual growth. The Spirit at work within us, by contrast, wants us to do and experience just the opposite.

Every person is born with a sin nature that can be called "the flesh." That's why no one has to teach a cherubic-looking four-year-old how to lie or do other naughty things like hitting his brother. Before coming to Christ, we are all enslaved to a desire to let that sin nature run things in our lives. But once we do place faith in Jesus, we get a new and far better nature. We get the Holy Spirit within us, and He is the One who prompts us to do right and empowers our efforts as we submit to God.[8] That's what it means to be born again! Now, once we get home to Heaven, we

---

[8] For more on this topic, see Romans 8:1–17.

will be perfect like Jesus—not divine, but sinless and free of the desire to sin. (Sin won't even exist where we're headed. Praise God!) Between now and then, we still have to live on this fallen planet. And as surely as the curse of Genesis 3:16–19 will age our bodies in spite of our coming to know Christ, that old sinful flesh nature that's been conquered in one sense will continue to try to influence us—to urge us to cozy up to the briar patch—until death. Thus we have a battle in our hearts. God wants us to be holy, increasingly like Jesus. The enemy wants us to be worldly, decidedly not like Christ.

> God wants us to be holy, increasingly like Jesus. The enemy wants us to be worldly, decidedly not like Christ.

The apostle Paul provides an important tool for recognizing whether the flesh or the Spirit of God holds the most sway over us. Consider these lists:

> The acts of the flesh are obvious: sexual immorality, impurity and debauchery; idolatry and witchcraft; hatred, discord, jealousy, fits of rage, selfish ambition, dissensions, factions and envy; drunkenness, orgies, and the like....
>
> But the fruit of the Spirit is love, joy, peace, forbearance, kindness, goodness, faithfulness, gentleness and self-control. (Galatians 5:19–23)

Evangelist R. A. Torrey made plain what it takes to produce the fruit of the Spirit. It boils down to abiding in Jesus. He said,

> To abide in Christ is to renounce any independent life of our own, and simply and constantly look to Christ to think His thoughts in us, to form His purposes in us, to feel His emotions and affections in us.... If we

are to obtain from God all that we ask of Him, Christ's words must abide or continue in us. We must study His words, let them sink into our thoughts and into our hearts, keep them in our memory, obey them constantly, let them shape and mold our daily life.[9]

It's in doing this that we choose holiness, that we keep God's Spirit, and not the flesh, on the throne of our hearts,[10] that we stay centered on the good path and stay away from the thorns.

Unfortunately, the world, which is still fully under the influence of the enemy, is strongly opposed to the idea of anyone living by the Spirit, of anyone actually becoming like Jesus. That's part of why Jesus said, "If the world hates you, keep in mind that it hated me first" (John 15:18). Yes, unbelievers might be drawn to benefits like peace and kindness that the Spirit produces in our hearts, but most assume anyone who actually prioritizes and emulates Jesus is either an ignorant fool or a religious extremist. So to suit their own preferences, they subtly encourage us believers to be just like them instead—to be lovers of self, lovers of pleasure, and lovers of things instead of lovers of our God. They emphasize finding joy and fulfillment in the pursuit of merely human relationships, gathering possessions, accumulating money, and indulging in food, sex, and self-advancement (compare this idea to what is said in 2 Timothy 3:1–5, 14–15). In his book *The Pursuit of God*, A. W. Tozer said this of the human heart's fleshly way of thinking and its effects: "God's gifts now take the place of God, and the whole course of nature is upset by this monstrous substitution."[11]

Indeed, choosing to indulge in worldliness instead of living for Christ, who came and took the death penalty that our personal

---

[9] R. A. Torrey and Stephen Johnson, *How to Pray: How to Study the Bible* (Peabody, MA: Hendrickson Publishers, 2011), 44.

[10] See the discussion in John 15:9–16.

[11] A. W. Tozer, *The Pursuit of God: The Definitive Classic* (Delight, AR: Gospel Light Publishing, 2013), 30.

sins earned us, is a "monstrous" way to "thank" Him for all He's done for us. So let's remember the apostle Paul's wisdom on this matter: "Let us keep in step with the Spirit" (Galatians 5:25).

In Timothy Jones's book *The Art of Prayer*, he states, "The Spirit is quenched by . . . excessive anxiety about worldly matters, by indulgence in sensual pleasures, by pandering to carnal desires, and by infatuation with material things. If this Spirit is quenched, then the Christian life will be quenched."[12] Let's be diligent to steer clear of the briar patch of worldly indulgence. And in the event that we run into it, let's immediately repent. As Proverbs 28:13 says, "Whoever confesses and turns away from his sins will find compassion and mercy" (AMP).

Theologian Warren Wiersbe gave us a lot of hope regarding this matter of our ability to prioritize the Lord over the long term despite the enemy's tactics. He said, "Once you have begun to cultivate this deeper communion with Christ, you will have no desire to return to the shallow life of a careless Christian."[13]

So, whether you think you are most likely to halt in your pursuit of spiritual growth because of doubts, distractions, busyness, fear, or even the flesh, stay focused on the rewards mentioned in the last chapter as well as on Jesus—the ultimate Reward! I don't want you to settle for anything else. You have the Holy Spirit in you, helping you "to will and to act in order to fulfill his good purpose" (Philippians 2:13). Further, you can "resist the devil," knowing that when you do, "he will flee" (James 4:7). And he'll have to take his tricks with him.

Give some thought to which of the road hazards discussed in this chapter is most likely to hinder you. Then take that matter to

---

[12] Timothy Jones, *The Art of Prayer: A Simple Guide to Conversation with God* (Milton Keynes, UK: Scripture Union Publishing, 2006), n.p. Kindle.

[13] Warren W. Wiersbe, *The Bible Exposition Commentary*, vol. 1 (Colorado Springs: David C. Cook, 2003), 355.

God in prayer, asking Him to strengthen you against it even now. He is so worth it!

TOPICAL REFLECTIONS

1. Which of the enemy road hazards Anita identified tends to be the most effective at hindering your spiritual walk? Why?

2. What specific doubts have you encountered in your walk? How have you dealt with them? What might you need to do differently the next time one arises?

3. What practical steps might you take to limit busyness and distractions in your life?

4. Basing your answer on Galatians 5:19–23, are you doing a better job of living in light of your spiritual nature or of your fleshly nature? What help does Proverbs 28:13 offer those Christ-followers who realize they're living according to the flesh?

5. Read what the apostle Paul had to say in 1 Corinthians 9:24–27. What encouragement or incentive for running hard in the spiritual race do you take from this? (Keep in mind that "the prize" in view is not entry into Heaven but hearing Jesus say, "Well done.")

CHAPTER 7

KEEP PURSUING GOD HIMSELF

"Am I seeking God for my own spiritual pleasure, or do I love Him for His own sake?"[1]

– R. C. Sproul

MY HUSBAND, PAUL, is a great and generous provider who excelled at his produce business, and I praise God for him all the time. Our grown children, with all their varied giftings, bring endless smiles and blessings into our lives, and I gratefully thank the Lord for them too. Twila—to my delight and amazement—is now a happy grandma herself, making me a great-grandmother twice over. That's another wonderful reason to praise! God has been so very gracious and good to me—in part through my connections to these precious family members! I really enjoy spending dedicated time with each one.

You certainly have people in your life you feel similarly grateful for and love spending time with. Imagine, though, how Paul would feel if I were to suddenly stop speaking to him as my much-loved husband and instead started treating him as nothing but the man who pays the bills and needs to be kept happy. How would my

---

[1] R. C. Sproul, *Enjoying God: Finding Hope in the Attributes of God* (Ada, MI: Baker Publishing Group, 2017), 134.

daughters and sons feel if my interest in their lives slowly ebbed away until only those happy occasions when one of them married or announced the coming of a new grandchild, and I wanted to be part of the excitement—or if I just stayed in touch with them out of a sense of duty? And do you think Twila would appreciate it if I bothered to check in with her only so I could have access to her children and grands—or if I was kind to her only out of obligation?

You know intuitively that I'd hurt my relationships with each of these people were I to start treating them in such ways—as surely as similar behavior coming from you would damage your own. No one, no matter how helpful and self-sacrificing in nature, likes to be used. Similarly, no one wants others to spend time with them simply to keep them appeased or because of obligation. We all want to be valued for who we are, not just what others can get from us. We want people to hang around us because they want to, not because they think they have to.

As we begin to wrap up our discussion of practical suggestions for seeking God faithfully, I want to touch on a few reminders that we all need. Even persistent seekers might occasionally send the Lord the message that they're slowly growing more interested in what He can do for them than they are in continuing to seek Him for Himself, or that they've ceased to spend time with Him out of a desire for closeness and are instead just trying to earn a little extra credit spiritually.

God does not need our interest or appreciation. He does not need us to fellowship with Him daily, much less want us to feel we have to. In fact, He needs nothing (see Psalm 50:9–13). Yet if we really think Him worthy, we will take care to approach Him with the right spirit. We'll remember to stay grateful for who He is and to remain in awe of the fact that He enjoys spending time with us. We will steadfastly pursue God Himself, nothing less—not even a desire for His approval.

Reminder 1: Having a Quiet Time Isn't a Requirement for Keeping God's Favor; He Doesn't Want Us to Think of It That Way.
On that morning when my family was visiting the little country church where the faithful elderly man with the breathing machine so blessed me, a younger man whose posture and demeanor suggested he dealt with some disabilities was sitting just ahead of us. I wouldn't have given him much notice had it not been for what happened during the worship service.

Throughout the sermon, the young man kept touching his face. The reason eventually became clear. In between rubbing and resting his eyes, he'd use his fingers to lift his lids as high as they would go. And then, when the pastor said something he found stirring, he'd excitedly yell, "JESUS!" and turn around to the rest of the congregation so we could see just how eye-opening he'd found the pastor's insights. The most incredible part of this was that no one else in the room—including the preacher—seemed to find it at all distracting. It was just me! Clearly, most were used to it. He was a loved and welcomed part of that local church. And they all knew he adored the Lord just as much as they, no matter the unique challenges he faced. He was expressing it in the only way he knew.

My heart lifted as I thought about that. Then something else occurred to me. That young man lacked the mental ability to do the kind of quiet-time routine I've found helpful in seeking intimacy with God. Yet the Lord, I knew from my study of the Word, was no less pleased with him and his childlike ways than He is when a gifted theologian seeks Him through putting in hours of in-depth Bible research. That young man is His dearly loved son through his simple faith in Jesus alone, as surely as I'm God's daughter for the same reason.

This, I think, serves as a beautiful reminder that the Lord really wants His people's hearts, not their academic efforts or habitual service to a program. So let's remain diligent about not allowing our quiet times to devolve into empty spiritual exercises we do out of mere routine or out of a misguided desire to please that have little to do with honoring God. How sad it would be if we who have the benefit of trusting directly in Jesus and having His Spirit within us followed the example of the people of Old Testament Judah. They did their religious rituals and offered sacrifices just as their ancestors had for generations, even though their hearts were anything but in them. God finally said this of the activities they privately felt were "a burden," something they did just to keep up appearances and to supposedly stay on God's good side: "A son honors his father, and a slave his master. If I am a father, where is the honor due me? If I am a master, where is the respect due me? . . . I am a great king" (Malachi 1:6, 13–14). In other words, He saw right through their actions to their bored hearts.

> Joyfully accept the responsibility of getting into the Word for yourself and diligently discovering firsthand what the Holy Spirit wants to teach you.

How tragic would it be if God had to ask the same thing about our half-hearted quiet times? Or how warped would it be if we were to start assuming that we are His favorites just because we clock in for those quiet times each day (see Romans 2:11)? What would that reveal about our level of trust in what Jesus accomplished for us on the cross (see Galatians 3:1–7)?

May we never be more interested in being able to claim, "I prayed and did my Bible reading today" than we are in actually engaging with God. In fact, if we do ever start to find ourselves thinking of quiet time that way, it's a sure sign we need to break things up, to take a weekend off and go for long walks during which we talk to and praise Him for His creations instead, to take hot bubble baths and sing His praises as we do. Or perhaps we should mix up our quiet times a little so that they feel less redundant.

When I find myself in a place of numbness or joylessness and need a reboot, I grab my cell phone and begin listening to my worship playlists on iTunes. Music has a beautiful way of drawing my heart back to God and the joy that comes from being in His presence as I worship Him in song. (My go-to songs at the moment are "He Is Worthy," "Way Maker," "Echo Holy," and "Move Your Heart.")

One of the best ways I've found to keep my quiet times from growing stale and to keep my heart in the posture it should have involves *detailed* joy-journaling; I'll discuss the concept at length in the next chapter. For now, know that something about doing it helps keep quiet time feeling less of a have-to and more of a want-to; it keeps my mind from disengaging from the wonderful joy of drawing closer to God.

I think this is a good spot to note that while there's nothing inherently wrong with using your quiet time to work your way through a devotional book or even a workbook Bible study, doing so can rob you of the adventure of getting to seek God for yourself. It really can make it feel more like a chore to get done. F. B. Meyer pointed out, "All sermons, all Bible classes, all religious magazines and books can never take the place of our own quiet study of God's precious Word"; acknowledging this is just what a journaling approach encourages.[2] By contrast, reading resources other than Scripture during the time you've set apart for closeness with the Father can make you numb to the awesome reality He wants you to learn from Him directly!

I love Christian resources. In fact, as you can see, I've written some. But these types of books and tools are authored by people who took the time to get alone with God, to read His Word, and to let the Holy Spirit teach them personally.[3] And that's a pow-

---

[2] Frederick Brotherton Meyer, *Steps into the Blessed Life* (Philadelphia: Henry Altemus, 1896), 287.

[3] In fact, famed evangelist John Wesley said, "I sit down alone; only God is here. In His presence I open, I read His book.... And what I thus learn, that I teach." John Wesley, *John Wesley* (Cary, NC: Oxford University Press, 1980), 89.

erful and exciting process I don't want you to miss out on! So, be aware that while working through such books is often a blessing, they should be read outside of quiet time. Joyfully accept the responsibility of getting into the Word for yourself and diligently discovering firsthand what the Holy Spirit wants to teach you.

This is as honoring to the Lord as when your teenager could Google for an answer but comes directly to you for advice instead! Yet I have no doubt He is equally pleased with you when you just give Him what you can, even if there are days when that's as simple as reverently whispering—or maybe even crying out—"JESUS!" because you feel you can do nothing more.

Reminder 2: Quiet Time Isn't a Session with Your Personal Genie.

Typically, those who spend daily, quality time with God have matured past the world's way of turning to Him only in times of crisis—as when many nonbelievers suddenly began filling America's churches in the wake of the 9/11 tragedy and then just stayed home again on Sundays when things started to feel more stable. As Francis Frangipane says, "[Spiritual] maturity starts as we break the cycle of seeking God only during hardship."[4]

Frangipane also says, "Holiness begins the moment we seek God for himself."[5] And the opposite is true, making this a good point at which to say that each of us must remain aware of just how easy it is to fall back into the world's way of thinking of God as a genie-on-call. Anyone who has been a persistent God-seeker for more than a short time knows that seeking Him for who He is and resting in that can be a pleasure when everything's going well. But when something bad suddenly happens, then something worse happens, and then we make a couple of sinful choices that

---

[4] Francis Frangipane, *Holiness, Truth, and the Presence of God: For Those Who Are Unsatisfied with Their Spiritual Life and Willing to Do Something about It* (Lake Mary, FL: Charisma House, 2011), 9.
[5] Ibid.

complicate things, we start to feel worn down, detached. It's then that the times we would normally spend in God's presence, just for the sake of being nearer to Him, can easily turn into sessions in which we spend the whole time crying out for God to fix the immediate problems just so we can move on with life as usual.

Oswald Chambers warned that while there is nothing wrong with seeking God's help in meeting life's trials (in fact, we should), "The point of prayer is not to get answers from God, but to have oneness with Him. If we only pray because we want answers, we will become irritated with God [should He fail to answer as we want]."[6]

God is worthy of a regular, focused investment of our time that can certainly include our honest reports of the tough things we are facing as well as requests for His help but that doesn't revolve around our demands that He swoop in and fix all that's difficult for us. To seek God for Himself means that I'm going to seek Him whether He answers my prayers or not, whether I feel His presence or not, whether I understand what I'm going through or not, or whether I feel my life is in order or not. I'm just going to show Him that I love and trust Him no matter what. Old Testament faith hero Job summed up just the radical attitude I want to have toward God when he said, "Though he slay me, yet will I hope in Him" (Job 13:15). Job mistakenly thought God was directly responsible for all the disasters that had recently befallen him, but he still chose to honor the Lord anyway! He felt it God's due and his own privilege.

I can testify that when you focus during quiet times on the Lord rather than your troubles, He will give you peace, and He will take care of you (see Isaiah 26:3). In His own perfect way, He will deliver—even if that means just providing you His peace as you keep journeying through that hard thing. Yet He will also do

---

[6] Oswald Chambers, *My Utmost for His Highest: Updated Language* (Grand Rapids: Our Daily Bread Publishing, 2010), n.p. Kindle.

something better. He will give you a deeper sense of who He is and how close He is at the same time. He will mature you in faith, as James 1:2–4 explains, which is a gift far greater than immediate release from a hardship. (Praise His holy name. I love Him so much!)

Reminder 3: Quiet Time Is Not the Time to Cram for the Bible Lesson You Will Teach Tomorrow.
Years ago I ran into a retired pastor I knew. We were both walking out to our cars in the bank's parking lot. We greeted each other warmly, and he asked what I'd been up to lately. I told him about my workshops designed to help people seek God.

He nodded in approval but didn't say a word for a long moment. Instead, he just stared at his shoes. Finally, he looked at me with a sad smile on his lined face and said, "Maybe this is a strange thing to hear an old preacher like me say, but one of my biggest regrets is that I didn't seek God more when I was younger and had more energy."

Of course, my response was to lightheartedly assure him that we can keep seeking God at every age. I am, after all, ever the cheerleader. But after we parted, I realized he'd actually admitted to something profound, something I needed to hear. Through his honesty, he'd urged me to think about this topic from a different and very important angle. That elderly former pastor had spent decades of his life leading God's people and teaching them Scripture—tasks that no doubt required him to spend countless hours in the Word and in prayer. Yet so much of that time he'd spent on accomplishing the right things for God, in preparation to better serve God, had failed to yield a sense of deep, personal intimacy with God. Rather, they'd just been the means to ends. He'd been looking for the right response to a question, figuring what passages the people most wanted to hear, and trying so hard to be prepared for ministry that he'd often neglected to spend time seeking God for the simple pleasure of doing so—as a way to honor Him and grow closer to Him at the same time, as I'm advocating. George Müller, a well-known theologian, gave us this warning: "Often the work of the Lord itself may tempt us away from communion with Him. A full schedule of preaching, counseling, and traveling can erode the strength of the mightiest servant of the Lord. Public prayer will never make up for the closet communion."[7]

The takeaway here is that we must remain careful not to let our study of Scripture for the sake of lesson or Bible quiz preparation intrude on our time with Jesus. How easy it is to assume because we are praying and studying the Word so we'll be ready to lead a small-group discussion or write a blog post that we are receiving all the nourishment our souls need, that we are actually seeking God even as we are seeking answers and preparation. But while it's true that 2 Timothy 2:15 urges us to be workers "who correctly handle the word of truth," and that does suggest there's a time to read Scripture as a student in training for fieldwork, that's no substitute for reading it simply to delight in God's presence because we desire closeness with Him. Phil Vischer, cocreator of *Veggie Tales*, wisely assures us, "The impact God has planned for you does not occur when you are pursuing impact; it occurs when you are pursuing God."[8]

While most of us wouldn't mind occasionally helping a friend study for a test or prepare to write a paper or deliver a speech, few of us would feel personally valued if asked to do it all the time and were otherwise ignored. As a parent, I'm thrilled when my kids come to me seeking help, but if occasions of need become the only times they come to me, I will feel used and hurt! Is it possible that when we choose to come to God only when we need His help,

---

[7] George Müller, *The Autobiography of George Müller* (Springdale, PA: Whitaker House, 1984), 47.

[8] Phil Vischer, quoted in Simon Guillebaud, Jan. 4 devotional, *365 Readings for Radical Disciples* (Oxford, UK: Lion Hudson Ltd., 2004), n.p. Kindle.

whether it's for ministry preparation or personal challenges we are facing, it hurts Him?

Over the last few years, a string of respected Christian leaders has experienced dramatic and very public tumbles into sin. I'm always saddened by such stories and have come to think of them as cautionary tales that lend support to my point in this section. Priest and author Henri Nouwen said it well: "Nothing conflicts with the love of Christ like service to Christ."[9] May you and I never get so busy doing ministry that we starve ourselves of the intimacy that comes from being alone with our Father just for the sake of spiritual nourishment and a desire to simply honor Him. It will only lead to unfortunate consequences.

AS WE DISCUSSED in chapter 5, there are all kinds of tremendous benefits that come from consistently seeking God. In fact, the honor of getting to approach Him as our Father is the greatest gift we could ever receive! So may we never settle for lesser things like feeling we have somehow further secured God's favor because we are checking the right spiritual activities boxes, or because during our quiet times we prep for the ministry work ahead with all the drive of a college student cramming for an exam. May we never fall back into treating God as merely our emergency line, subconsciously hoping He'll come through for us the next time if we'll just keep showing up in the slot we've set aside to spend with Him each day.

Closeness with God—all by itself—is a beautiful thing, *the* goal I'm advocating! Something we must decide not only to aim for but to cherish and protect for the long term.

You know, there was a time when I'd think of preachers and Bible study writers as Christians who had "arrived" while the rest

---

[9] Henri Nouwen, quoted in Dallas Willard, *The Great Omission: Reclaiming Jesus's Essential Teachings on Discipleship* (New York: HarperCollins, 2006), 94.

of us could only look on with awe. Their closeness with God was an alien concept to me personally. Yet time and experience have revealed that the only real difference between them and me boiled down to their ongoing decision to prioritize seeking God for the simple fact that He is worthy of the effort—that there is nothing better than being in fellowship with Him.

A. W. Tozer apparently once thought of Bible heroes with this same sense of awe I've described and wisely drew a similar conclusion about them. He said,

> Go back to the Word of God and consider how thirsty the friends of God were for God Himself. The great difference between us and Abraham, David, and Paul is that they sought Him and found Him and seeking Him still, found Him and sought Him continually. We accept Him and seek Him no more and that is the difference.[10]

The fact that you are still reading this book suggests you want to be an exception to the unfortunate norm Tozer identified. So spend the next few moments asking the Lord to help you stay fired up about seeking Him wholeheartedly and for all the right reasons. And know that I am cheering you on.

---

[10] James L. Snyder and A. W. Tozer, *Tozer on Worship and Entertainment* (Chicago: Moody Publishers, 2006), n.p. Kindle.

TOPICAL REFLECTIONS

1. Think back to when you picked up this book about seeking God. What were your initial reasons for wanting to learn about this topic? What, if anything, has changed?

2. Read Malachi 1:6, 13–14. What, according to Anita's reminders above, are three things we can avoid doing regarding quiet time to keep from similarly showing contempt for God's name?

3. What is the difference between going to God and asking His help in dealing with troubles versus treating Him like a genie?

4. How can you guard against letting preparation for the work of the Lord get in the way of seeking Him?

5. Billy Graham said, "We must read the Bible as men and women seeking God."[11] What evidence could you give to prove that you consistently approach quiet times this way?

---

[11] Russ Busby, *Billy Graham, God's Ambassador: A Lifelong Mission of Giving Hope to the World* (Fairfax, VA: TimeLife Books, 1999), 27.

CHAPTER 8

TAKE THE 21-DAY CHALLENGE

"It has been my habit to read the Bible through four times a year; in a prayerful spirit, to apply it to my heart, and practice what I find there. I have been for sixty-nine years a happy man; happy, happy, happy."[1]
– George Müller

IT HAS BEEN my joy and privilege sharing the JoyShop message with *you*. What a gift to be able to encourage and help equip you in your walk with our wonderful Lord! I am super excited for you too because I know that as you consistently choose to prioritize time in God's Word, you will be beautifully transformed. It can't be helped. Yes, for you—particularly if you are new to personal Bible study—there are positive changes ahead: powerful shifts in how you do life at home, at church, at school, or where you work; and in how you think, speak, and act. And as for those you encounter? Well, the more time you spend with Jesus and the better you get to know His Word, the more likely you are to talk about Him and to let people see what it's like when a woman gives herself fully to the most important relationship she will ever have.

With confidence, I can say great things are ahead for you!

---

[1] George Müller, quoted in Henry Hampton Halley, *Halley's Bible Handbook with the New International Version* (Grand Rapids: Zondervan, 2012), 807.

Back in chapter 4 I promised to share with you the specific routine I've developed for use in my own quiet times, what I do to bring structure and depth to those daily minutes that seem to fly by as I sit with my Bible open. This too is a simple method, certainly not magical or meant to be taken as the only way to rightly seek God through Scripture. But I'm convinced that if you'll give it a try, it really will help arm you to walk through every book of the Bible on your own.[2] I'm also hopeful that as you experience the joy of His presence, it will give you a stronger desire to keep reading it through and sharing Scripture with others for the rest of your years. Since God's Word is "alive and active," it has the remarkable ability to "adapt [itself] to your spiritual level"[3] (see Hebrews 4:12). That means that while the words are changeless, they can impact you differently every time you read them with a teachable heart. Isn't that exciting?

Now, to begin, I'll share the steps of the routine I've promised. After that, I'll present to you a challenge that can't help but get you—and those in your Bible study group, if you've been meeting with one in relation to this book—off to a strong run at seeking God regularly and with joyful focus.

The Plan

My hope is that you've been reading a chapter of Proverbs each morning for a while now. I say that because having done so will prove an excellent warm-up to what I'll propose here. But whether or not you've been reading Proverbs alongside the latter half of this book as prompted in chapter 4, please grab your Bible and turn to it now. Flip to Proverbs 31.

---

[2] You may, however, want to work your way up to the more complex books like Revelation.

[3] Jeanne Guyon and Gene Edwards, *Intimacy with Christ* (Jacksonville, FL: The SeedSowers, 2001), 61.

1. Ask God what He wants you to know.

The first step of this method is all about humility and choosing to invite the Lord into quiet times, something I feel is deeply important. So with your Bible in your lap—before you read anything—ask, "Father, will You please show me what You want me to see in the passage I'm about to study? Will You please speak to me through it and help me hear from You today? I really want to know You and obey You" (see John 8:55).

In John 14:26 Jesus said to His disciples, "The Holy Spirit, whom the Father will send in my name, will teach you all things and will remind you of everything I have said to you." In asking God for His help in terms of processing what you'll read in Scripture, you demonstrate that you welcome that same Spirit to teach you and to help you connect the dots between what you've already learned about the Lord and His will with what you need to hear next. You are also getting out of the way. You are choosing, as theologian A. W. Tozer urged, not to "come [to the Bible] with the notion it is a thing which you may push around at your convenience."[4] Rather, you are approaching it with an open mind that accepts it as the divine truth it is.

Take a moment now to ask God what He wants you to know about Proverbs 31. Invite His Holy Spirit to be in charge of this practice quiet time.

2. Read the day's passage.

I say "passage" and not "chapter" here because I always want you to read however much of Scripture you can truly process within whatever time frame you've allotted.[5] Your quiet time will look

---

[4] A. W. Tozer, *The Pursuit of God Updated Edition* (Alexandria, VA: Life Sentence Publishing, 2015), 61.

[5] Following the challenge I'll propose, what passage of Scripture you choose to study next will be up to you. Popular approaches include reading straight through the New Testament, reading through the Bible from cover to cover, or reading through it with the help of a chronologically ordered Bible reading plan. My favorite of these is called *The Victory Bible Reading Plan*, by James McKeever. https://www.amazon.com/Victory-Bible-Reading-James-McKeever/dp/0866941029

different from everyone else's, even if you are in a group of close friends who are all generally following my proposed plan; that's okay. Slower readers, for example, may not always be able to get through a whole chapter quickly enough to engage with it within a half hour. Speedy readers may be able to take in multiple chapters in even a fifteen-minute sitting, and I don't want to frustrate them. So whether you choose to read a whole chapter at a time, a small book of Scripture, or only a little section of a chapter, know that the goal I advocate is simply to take your time reading through whatever passage you've chosen.

> Always try to look at a Bible passage as if it's the first time you've ever seen it.

I want you to go to the Bible every day as if you are eager and focused on the love letter God has sent you. Ideally, in fact, I'd like you to always try to look at a passage as if it's the first time you've ever seen it. (And perhaps that's indeed the case.) But whether we have read a passage of Scripture one hundred times or it's completely new to us, our reading with fresh eyes allows the Lord to show us spiritual truths in a new light. In taking our time, in refusing to think we already know all there is to know about a passage, we are once again demonstrating humility and showing the Father that we truly want the Holy Spirit to speak to our hearts.

What proves very helpful to me in this step is bringing a highlighter to quiet time. (Crayon pencils are great and inexpensive study tools, by the way, since they won't bleed through a traditional Bible's thin pages). Highlighters equip you to mark things that stand out to you as you do an initial read. You can write in your Bible's margins too, perhaps starring things that grab your attention and briefly noting why. (I have met women who don't feel comfortable marking in their Bibles, and if that is you, no worries! You can ignore this suggestion. Or you could experiment and buy an inexpensive Bible and try highlighting in that one for your devotional time.)

Pens and highlighters are the fanciest study tools I'll advocate for this particular quiet-time approach. We don't need academic Bible resources stacked near our chairs or available on our phones. Naturally, Bible margin notes and articles can be helpful, and commentaries and good illustrated Bible dictionaries can be too. But I am convinced that there is nothing more beneficial to a believer's walk than just engaging with the Word itself. John Bunyan, author of the highly acclaimed allegory *Pilgrim's Progress*, did not have much education in the traditional sense. Yet as his famous story about the Christian pilgrim's life proves, he nevertheless had an excellent handle on God's truth. That's because he was a man totally dedicated to studying the Word for himself.[6] To believers just like you and me, he said this about the Bible:

> Read and read again and do not despair of help to understand the will and mind of God though you think they are fast locked up from you. Neither trouble your heads though you have not commentaries and expositions. Pray and read. Read and pray. For a little from God is better than a great deal from men. There is nothing that so abides with us as what we receive from God.[7]

So, let's get going! Take a few minutes to read slowly through Proverbs 31. And if you have a highlighter or pen handy, mark the verses that stand out to you—whatever the reason.

---

[6] For more on Bunyan, see "John Bunyan," *Banner Authors. Banner of Truth*: https://banneroftruth.org/us/about/banner-authors/john-bunyan/ (May 4, 2021).

[7] John Bunyan and George Whitfield, *The Works of that Eminent Servant of Christ, Mr. John Bunyan: Late Minister Of The Gospel And Pastor Of The Congregation At Bedford* (W. Johnston, 1768), 213.

3. Take time to reflect on what you've just read.
Did you ever have one of those teachers or professors who was forever offering not one-size-fits-all homework assignments but rather several potential daily options from which you could select? If so, you already know that having options can help you engage and keep study from growing stale. In the reflection phase of my routine, I focus on detailed journaling: Joy Journaling. But—as I'll outline below—I get to choose what I do within each journaling session. I've found that the practice of copying quotes from my Bible reading, jotting down my personal responses to what I've read, and even trying to describe my feelings help "to bring a [deeper] sense of reality" and intimacy "to [my] relationship with our invisible God."[8] It helps bring clarity to my heart about what I've read. And an added bonus I've discovered is that when I flip back through an old quiet-time journal, even years after I've shelved it, I can see hard evidence of how I've grown in understanding and faith. In a sense, then, journaling serves as a written record of what God is doing in my life.

Truth be known, I still don't particularly like to write things out, mainly because my handwriting is horrible and it's time-consuming. I have a bad habit of always being in a hurry, and journaling requires some patience. In the old days I'd trim my time working at it to the bare minimum. I'd scratch something illegible down and say, "That's good. I'm ready to go." But what I've discovered is that as surely as there's a difference between merely reading the Word and intently listening to it, there's a difference between journaling just to get it done and journaling as a means of giving thoughtful response to God, who has generously entrusted His Word to us. "A journal," Bible professor Donald S. Whitney says, "is a place where we give expression to the fountain of our hearts, where we can unreservedly pour out our passion before the

---

[8] Bruce Wilkinson, *Secrets of the Vine: Breaking through to Abundance* (England: Crown Publishing Group, 2012), 109.

Lord."[9] So I encourage you to make time to journal thoughtfully and completely—even if that means you do so on an electronic tablet or laptop.

What are the varied options to approaching this journaling section of quiet time? The following are the ideas I've found most helpful. I'll write them as do-steps for easy reference, but please remember that you are not stuck with my ideas. You are welcome to adjust or add to these as you like.

a. *Consider the verses you highlighted during your reading. Then write down a favorite or two, along with why you think each one spoke to you.* Don't over-spiritualize. Rather, ask and answer questions like these: What lesson(s) does this teach? How does this challenge me? What's beautiful about it? Why did I rejoice or perhaps recoil when I encountered it?

b. *Think about what the whole passage (or a part of it) revealed to you about God, and write it and your related thoughts down. Tell the Lord your feelings on that revelation.*

c. *Ask yourself, What does the Lord want me to do with what I've read? Then write both the answer and how you might act on it.*

d. *Scan the biblical text a second time, looking for repeated words, phrases, or concepts within it.* (For instance, I always circle the word *heart* when I find it in the Bible. It's a noun that grabs my attention because I want to know what God has to say about my heart.) *Write down the repeats or mentions of common biblical inclusions like "heart" that you'd like to trace personally. Then explain what you gain from the latest mentions you noted.*

---

[9] Donald S. Whitney, *Spiritual Disciplines for the Christian Life* (Colorado Springs: NavPress, 2014), 255.

e. *Look back at verses you highlighted and choose one to memorize. Write down why you'd like to commit it to memory and then copy the passage three times to help with that effort.*[10]

f. *Scan the section you read for what I call "wow passages." That is, look for statements within the text that wow you, that would prove revolutionary to your walk with the Lord were you to truly believe them. So often, we say, "Of course I believe all the promises in the Bible!" Yet have you ever noticed how much easier it is to believe a promise for someone else who is going through a difficult time than for yourself when faced with a situation that looks impossible? I have found that I need to be deliberate in focusing on the promises found in God's Word so I can apply them to my own life. Copy down each wow passage and write about why it challenges or encourages you. Explain what would change if you actually took it to heart.*

There's a section in Jeremiah in which God prompts His prophet to "Write in a book all the words [He has] spoken to [him]" (Jeremiah 30:2). It's my belief that writing down portions of Scripture yourself as well as recording what God has spoken to your heart through them is an excellent way to help you remember what *He* wants you to do.

Now, will you please grab your Joy Journal and select one, several, or even all of the above options and apply it to Proverbs 31?[11] In his book *Enjoying God*, R. C. Sproul urges us to "Write honestly and deeply about the things [we] feel the Holy Spirit is speaking to [our hearts]" and to "Be . . . reflective."[12] You may be pleasantly surprised by what comes of it.

---

[10] I prefer to keep a separate, index-card-sized spiral notebook handy for this purpose. I write passages I want to memorize inside it so I can keep them in my pocketbook and study them during wait times.

[11] Please remember you are always welcome to use as many or as few of these options as you like. There is no rule to this. Be you.

[12] R. C. Sproul, *Enjoying God: Finding Hope in the Attributes of God* (Ada, MI: Baker Publishing

BEFORE MOVING FORWARD, I'd like to share a personal story about how God used this method of reflecting on His Word to equip me for something He knew I'd soon encounter. I bring this up here to help you see that the effort I'm urging you to expend will not be wasted. In fact, it just might lead not only to the rewards already discussed but also to tangible personal victories that are currently unimaginable.

I'd been following my quiet-time routine for several years when I was invited to speak at a local college's morning chapel. I knew there'd be about seventeen hundred students there, and I wanted to share with them my story and message related to Twila's file in hopes of drawing at least a few of them to my evening campus workshop. On that particular occasion, though, I was afraid. Why? Well, for one thing, the campus had offered me only a very small room and only two hours during which to give my JoyShop presentation that evening; those decisions made it clear that they expected the majority of the students would lack interest or be too busy to attend. Even more paralyzing was that I remembered what I and many of my college friends had done back during chapel hours. We'd snuck in a little study time or dozed through many of them. We'd rarely listened to the non-captivating speakers. Therefore, I reasoned, I'd probably find myself talking to nearly two thousand bored young people who'd completely tune me out, which meant that most likely few would bother to attend the workshop I offered.

As I drove to the campus battling discouragement, I started thinking about many of the wonderful things God had revealed to me during our morning times together, deeply wishing I could somehow help the students get a sense of just how awesome it is to really get to know the Father through His Word. It wasn't long

---

Group, 2017), 155.

before I began smiling to myself over several wow passages God had shown me. One of them was John 15:7: "If you remain in me and my words remain in you, ask whatever you wish, and it will be done for you."

That particular verse totally gripped my heart as I pulled into the school's parking lot. I said it aloud—several times. Then I started to pray it: "Heavenly Father, I remember that You have taught me in Your Word that since I am in You through Christ and am allowing Your Word to remain in and influence me, I can ask whatever I want and You will give lavishly as I ask not in selfishness but according to Your will [see James 4:3]. So Lord, I'm asking You to please help me be engaging as I share my story this morning. Please help the students, all of whom You long to draw closer, to listen and even to be motivated to check out the workshop tonight. You know how very much I want to encourage them to get into Your Word. I praise and thank You. In Jesus's name."

Hours later, not only had I gotten through my chapel message—during which I could see most students were actually listening to me with rapt attention (praise the Lord!)—but I also had the joy of witnessing two-hundred-plus students showing up so that the school had to relocate the workshop to a larger facility! I am convinced it was having memorized, actually believing, and choosing to act on that wow passage I'd encountered during a quiet time that led to that amazing opportunity. A powerful occasion the Lord used for His own glory and the good of His much-loved children.

4. Don't forget to respond directly to God for what He showed you during quiet time.
The response segment of my quiet times is the immediate application phase. Ideally, I will continue to respond to what God shows me long after I get up from a seeking session. Nevertheless, this part of the routine is, I think, the most exciting of all, the most

life-changing. It's all about taking what we've gained from God within His Word and showing Him that we're actively receiving it. A simple acronym, POWER, will help you understand what I mean. To close each quiet time, I ...

> **P**ray God's Word back to Him.
> **O**bey what He's told me to do to the extent I can in the moment.
> **W**orship Him with praise and thanksgiving.
> **E**xpect Him to answer my prayer related to His Word.
> **R**epent of any wrong attitude or action revealed by my most recent study of Scripture.

Let me walk you through these points in some detail. (My hope is that you'll apply them to what you've read in Proverbs 31 as we go.)

First, praying God's Word back to Him simply refers to talking to God about something you read during quiet time, whether you do that aloud, silently, or through a note you pen to Him in your Joy Journal. For me, this often looks something like this: I just say, "God, thank You for this Word about such-and-such today. Thank You for reminding me that ... or for showing me that I need to ... I like how Your Word says ...."

Do whatever is most comfortable for you, whatever best fits the passage you've read, but never be afraid to proclaim the Lord's promises and provisions out loud. The goal of this step is to talk to God specifically about something He revealed to you as you sat at His feet. You are signaling to Him a willingness to receive His investment into your heart.

Obeying what God told you, by extension, is exactly what it sounds like. If a section of Scripture made you think, *Oh, I really should do a better job of that!* or if encountering the Word for yourself revealed that your thinking was off at some point, go ahead and ask God to help you realign your life and thoughts with His. For me, this often starts with another prayer, like this: "God, I didn't realize that You want me to . . . I've got a long track record of doing just the opposite. Will You please help me to obey what I sense You are telling me to do here, or will You please help change my thinking so I can better align with Your will on this point?" Then I go ahead and act on it to whatever extent I can.

Let's consider this step in relation to the Proverbs passage. If Proverbs 31:12, which says a wife of noble character "brings [her husband] good, not harm, all the days of her life," causes me to realize I've been nagging my own husband lately, that's a sign the Holy Spirit is at work on my heart through my engagement with His Word. So I don't just push past the feeling. Rather, I obey His nudge by sending my man a quick text to apologize, to tell him I appreciate him, and to ask his forgiveness for my impatient mouth. (There's no need for self-condemnation here or anywhere else. First Corinthians 10:13 says, "No temptation has overtaken [us] except that which is common to mankind." So let's remember grace!)

Or maybe last night I got sucked into the bad habit of spending a significant portion of my evening scrolling through social media platforms. Before I knew it, I'd spent an hour looking at all the wonderful happenings in others' lives. Then today, as I am reading through Proverbs 31, verse 27 jumps off the page and right into my heart, convicting me that I eat a lot of "the bread of idleness" when I am visiting all my social media accounts that are so easily accessible on my phone. When these moments nudging me to repentance come, I ask God to give me a doable plan to make the changes necessary not to give into temptation. (For instance, I could remove the social media apps from my phone.)

After my initial obedience step, even if it's as simple as jotting myself a note to take a specific decisive action once I get up, it's time to worship, to let go of any stress (or unnecessary guilt) my act of obedience caused or might cause me and to just re-center on the Lord, who loves me so very much. So whether it's directly motivated by something you read or not, whether you want to listen to a little praise music while you engage in it or not, I hope you'll just take a moment or two to worship Him at this point in the routine, to praise God for who He is and what He's done for you. And if He revealed something particularly inspiring to you during your reading time, make sure to thank Him for that too. (Who doesn't like to receive a thank-you note for a generous gift supplied?)

Once my own brief sessions of worship conclude, I let the Lord know I have an attitude of expectation where He and His promises are concerned. Depending on what I've read, I might thank Him once again that He has promised "never [to] leave [me] or forsake [me]" (Deuteronomy 31:6; Hebrews 13:5), that He is my Provider (Philippians 4:19), and that I will one day have the privilege of spending eternity with Him. I might praise Him for making me ever more like Jesus (Romans 8:29). Yes, sometimes my expressions of expectancy sound hyper-focused on my daily reading, like this: "Father, I just read in Scripture that . . . , so I am trusting that You will . . ." Or maybe I say, "Now, Lord, I just read that You want me to . . . Honestly, that still sounds a little foreign to me, so I ask Your help in believing that and letting it change me." Or if I've come across a super-challenging verse that I don't know how to process, I go ahead and thank Him that His Word is true and perfect whether or not I always grasp it. And I ask Him to help me stand on what I do know and—if it is His will—to reveal more to me about that hard passage I don't quite understand. Then I trust that He will answer that prayer in His own perfect timing.

Finally, I close out my quiet time with any repentance needed to reinforce my commitment to fully obey whatever He's told me to do. In this step, I'm not thinking in terms of recent and willful sins, though repenting of those is a natural part of seeking God, as we've discussed. At this point, I'm talking about truly and verbally repenting of any actions or attitudes that my most recent session in the Word has revealed to me are wrong.

For instance, let's say I've been reading the book of Exodus, and today I read Exodus 20. One verse I highlighted was Exodus 20:7: "You shall not misuse the name of the Lord your God, for the Lord will not hold anyone guiltless who misuses His name." If prior to today's read, I've been casually using God's name in a culturally familiar exclamation of surprise—even if only in abbreviated form—my latest encounter with the Word begs me to make a course correction. No, the Lord doesn't want me to panic and beat myself up over my newly realized sin. Rather, He wants me to repent of it and trust that Jesus died to cover that too. And moving forward, He wants me to begin making a sincere effort to steer away from what may have become a comfortable bad habit.

Daily engaging with God's Word, even if you've been a Christ-follower for decades, will sometimes expose areas that require repentance and the need to make a change. It may even ask you to revisit your beliefs on certain subjects you didn't even know Scripture speaks to. When the Holy Spirit shines His light onto some sin you're committing—like indulging beliefs that run counter to Scripture—please don't see the revelation as a bad thing. It's not a realization to feel miserably guilty about, get defensive over, or run from. It's an opportunity to obediently join with the Father as He works to make you more like Jesus, absolutely lovely through and through.

The 21-Day Challenge

My prayer is that you'll close this book with a determination to apply the above seeking routine, starting tomorrow. Ideally, I'd like you to begin with a three-week test run through the Gospel of John. In my workshops I refer to it as "the 21-Day Challenge." Not only is that particular Bible book a favorite of mine, but it does an excellent job of helping us really get to know Jesus better through the written memories of one who walked alongside Him for three years. John the apostle, one of only three disciples among Jesus's inner circle and not to be confused with John the Baptist, was so touched—so overcome—that the Son of God had chosen him that he rarely referred to himself by name when talking about Him. Often within the text, John just called himself "the disciple whom Jesus loved," a phrase expressing John's amazement over Christ's affection toward him.[13] John was so blown away that he'd been allowed the privilege of walking alongside His Creator physically that he rightly introduced Jesus first not by name but as "the Word ... with God [even] in the beginning" (John 1:1–2).[14]

Whether you'll be approaching John's Gospel for the first time this week or know the book well, I'm so hopeful you will choose to see it for what it really is: part of God's sixty-six-book love letter to you, a personal account overseen by the Lord and passed down through many generations so that *you* might study it and get to know Him through it, so that you too can come to see yourself as a disciple Jesus truly loves—and boldly live in light of it![15]

---

[13] John 13:23; 19:26; 21:7, 20.

[14] Compare this with the *us* and *our* in Genesis 1:26–27.

[15] In preparation for sharing what you learn from John with others, consider ordering pocket-sized editions of that Gospel. I find these to be excellent tools not only for discipling other believers but also in confidently sharing my faith with unbelievers. Visit www.ptl.org to become a member of the Pocket Testament League and have copies shipped to you. You'll be able to select your preferred cover design, Bible version, and print size.

DAILY STEPS TO BE FOLLOWED IN THE 21-DAY CHALLENGE

1. *Pray, asking God what He wants you to know about Him and His will in the passage you're about to read.*
2. *Read the day's passage, using a highlighter to note things that stand out.*
3. *Take time to reflect on what you've read by choosing one joy-journaling option or several:*
    a. Consider each verse you highlighted, write down favorites, and explain why you think each spoke to you.
    b. Write down what you just learned about God as well as your feelings on that.
    c. Ask yourself, What does the Lord want me to do with what I've just read? Then write both the answer and actions you might take to apply it.
    d. Scan the text again for repeated words, phrases, or Bible terms that catch your attention. Explain what you gain from their inclusion in the passage.
    e. Scan the verses you highlighted and select one to memorize: write down why you chose it and copy it three times.
    f. Review the text you read, looking for "wow passages." Copy each one and write about why it challenges or encourages you. Write about what would change if you actually took it to heart.
4. *Don't forget to respond directly to God for what He showed you during quiet time:*
    Pray God's Word back to Him.
    Obey what He's told you to do to the extent you can in the moment.
    Worship Him with praise and thanksgiving.
    Expect Him to answer your prayer related to His Word.
    Repent of any wrong attitude or action revealed by your study of Scripture.

LEADER'S GUIDE

WELCOME! THANK YOU so much for choosing to walk alongside and encourage others in the faith over the course of these next weeks. The following information will help you plan and lead your own small-group study of *Seeking God First: A Practical Plan for Finding Joy and Peace in Him*. Questions and activities for a total of eight sessions are included.[1] Allow for a week of reading time prior to each meeting.

Before Session 1
1. Pray, inviting the Lord to bring to your group exactly those He knows will benefit from it most. Ask Him to prepare their hearts and to give you sincere love for each woman you'll lead in the weeks ahead.
2. Select your meeting space and time and announce it to those who might participate in the group with you. (Bonus points if you speak with each one in person rather than just texting or inviting her via announcements at church.) Make sure to tell every individual how excited you are at the thought of learning and growing alongside her.
3. Whether you'll be leading in your living room, a coffee shop, or a church classroom, consider what you might

---

[1] Please note that while the content of this study was developed from Anita's "Discovering the Joy of Seeking God First" video content, those films do not follow the chronology of this resource and are not a necessary component of it.

do to make that area as homey and inviting as possible. You may, for instance, choose to welcome everyone to the first meeting with homemade cookies and a spiral-bound, lined journal (a Joy Journal) she can use later in the course.
4. Ensure that every participant has a copy of this book. ***The Introduction and Chapter 1 will need to be read before the first meeting. Encourage participants to highlight what stands out to them and to jot down their answers to the Topical Reflection questions;*** you'll sometimes reference them during the group sessions.
5. Purchase ink pens and lined index cards that can be used during group time; these tools will be used throughout the study.

SESSION 1

(A discussion of what was read in the introduction and chapter 1)

1. Begin on time.
   - Warmly welcome participants: offer goodie bags and/or baked goods if you choose.
   - Open in prayer.
2. Introduce yourself.
   - Ask participants to do the same by sharing three fun or humorous personal facts. (Begin by sharing your own; for instance, *I'm a rollercoaster fan; it's my dream to go to Ireland one day; and I'm afraid of frogs.*)
3. Pass out index cards and ask participants to join you in anonymously jotting down what they hope to get out of the study.
   - Take the cards up and then read them aloud with your own, taking care not to reveal who said what.
   - Express enthusiasm over the thought of seeing the Lord answer these hopes in the weeks ahead.
4. Request that volunteers who are willing to share their testimonies explain how and why they came to place faith in Jesus.
   - After each share, thank the speaker for being brave. Then ask, What letter grade, or grade range, would you assign yourself to represent how faithfully you've sought the Lord and lived for Him since first trusting in Christ?
   - Share your own story about how you came to faith in Jesus, being brutally honest about how well you've sought Him since.
   - Express that the point of this grading exercise is to acknowledge that even faithful, committed Christians—like the apostle Peter, who denied Christ three times—sometimes fall on their faces spiritually and need encouragement in staying the course.

- Note joyfully that the great news is that you are all poised to seek Him much more diligently for having walked through this study together.
5. Ask, What consequences did Anita run into out of her teenage failure to seek the Lord post-salvation?
   - Ask, What consequences did she run into out of her failure to seek the Lord consistently later in life?
   - Ask, What specific frustrations do you think you've encountered as a result of going your own way rather than continuing to pursue closeness with God post-salvation?
   - Ask, Do you think God allows us to experience consequences for our sinful actions out of anger or in hopes of urging us back on track? Explain your answer.
6. Ask participants to share how they saw God at work in Anita's life in spite of her seasons of rebellion.
   - Encourage them to share about times when they've seen God working to draw them back to His side in spite of their own rebelliousness.
7. Have all participants turn to p. 24 for their answers to chapter 1's Topical Reflections questions.
   - Request that a volunteer read aloud 1 John 1:6–10.
   - Ask, What convicted you in that passage? What brought comfort?
8. Ask for a volunteer to explain why humble repentance is so key to seeking God.
9. Ask participants to share what they highlighted or found most meaningful as they read the introduction and chapter 1.
10. Assign the reading of chapter 2, making sure to clarify the next meeting's date and time.
11. Close in prayer.

SESSION 2

(A discussion of what was read in chapter 2)

1. Begin on time.
   - Open in prayer. Thank the Lord for each participant by name if possible.
2. Request that a volunteer read the first sentence of 1 Chronicles 22:19 (NIV).
   - Ask the group, What did devoting your heart to seeking God look like to you before we began this study?
   - Ask, Do you think most Christians think of devoting oneself to God as something they can do personally, or do you think most assume such devotion is only for people like pastors, priests, and deacons? Explain your answer.
3. Point out that in Psalm 119:10–16 we learn about what seeking the Lord looked like for David.
   - Encourage all participants to turn to it in their Bibles and then ask, What bearing, if any, do you think what David revealed here had on why God called him "a man after his own heart" in 1 Samuel 13:14?
   - Ask, What implications might we draw from this?
4. Encourage participants to respond to the idea that the Bible is essentially a file of information God wants us—His children—to have.
   - Ask for volunteers to look up and read the following verses from God's file to His kids' hearts:
     - Romans 5:6–8
     - Ephesians 2:4–10
     - Ephesians 5:1–2
     - Galatians 2:20
     - 1 John 3:1–3
     - 1 John 4:7–11, 16
     - Romans 8:37–40

> Ask, What's your favorite takeaway from these passages?
5. Ask, Why, according to chapter 2, is it important that we read our Bibles daily and not just every once in a while?
   - Why do you think God allows us to explore or neglect His Word rather than *insisting* we memorize and live by it faithfully?
6. Have everyone turn to pp. 33–34.
   - Ask, Which of the verses about the blessings of seeking God most stood out to you?
   - Ask, How have you seen one of these prove true in your own life?
7. Ask participants to share what they highlighted or found meaningful in chapter 2.
8. Assign the reading of chapter 3 and close in prayer.

SESSION 3
(A discussion of what was read in chapter 3)

1. Begin on time.
   - Open in prayer, thanking God for the awesome blessing of being able to speak to Him directly.
2. Request that a volunteer read the opening header quote of chapter 3 (p. 39).
   - Ask, Why do you think famed evangelist Billy Graham, a man who shared the gospel with millions all over the world, felt he should've prayed more?
   - Ask, What might Graham's words imply about how important prayer is in the life of the average Christ-follower?
3. Have all participants turn to p. 54 for their answers to chapter 3's Topical Reflections questions.
   - Ask, What does the phrase "the dual nature of humanity" refer to?
   - Ask, Why are the body and soul equally important, and why should each be nourished?
4. Ask, Why, according to this chapter, is it important that we pray continuously and not just every once in a while?
   - Ask, On a scale of 1–10, with 1 meaning "almost never" and 10 meaning "almost constantly," how consistently do you typically pray?
   - Ask, Why do you think most believers typically pray only now and then?
5. Read aloud the following four "I am" statements Jesus made, encouraging participants to listen in such a way as to identify their favorites:
   - *In John 6:35 Jesus said, "I am the bread of life. He who comes to Me shall never hunger, and he who believes in Me shall never thirst" (NKJV).*

- *In John 8:12 Jesus said, "I am the light of the world. He who follows Me shall not walk in darkness, but have the light of life" (NKJV).*
- *In John 11:25 Jesus said, "I am the resurrection and the life. He who believes in Me, though he may die, he shall live" (NKJV).*
- *In John 14:6 Jesus said, "I am the way, the truth, and the life. No one comes to the Father except through Me" (NKJV).*
  - Ask each participant individually, Which of these statements most stood out to you: the one about bread, light, life, or the way and truth? Explain.
  - Ask, Why might memorizing your favorite "I am" passage help you remember to pray more consistently?
    › Pass out index cards and encourage participants to write out their favorite of the four verses and pin it up in a prominent place in their home as a call to prayer.
6. Have participants scan the sample prayers from the Bible recorded on pp. 43–44. Ask which ones most encouraged them and why.
7. Request that a volunteer define "MBM prayers."
   - Note that it might prove helpful to get a little practice with this idea. Select various participants to suggest what an MBM prayer might sound like in each of the following situations:
     - You wake up feeling so discouraged that you don't want to get out of bed.
     - You look out the window to see it's a gloriously beautiful morning.
     - Your child is disrespectful.
     - You learn that your best friend definitely does not have the scary thing her doctor thought she might.
     - You hear that they are about to lay people off at work.
     - Your husband receives an unexpected promotion.

> Ask, Why do you think we were given as many positive opportunity-to-pray examples as negative ones here?
8. Ask, What did the story of how Anita's response to her injured son's faint cry contribute to the chapter's discussion of prayer?
9. Note that Anita taught about how dissatisfaction, loneliness, restlessness, weakness, and brokenness can all indicate we are depriving ourselves of spending enough time with God in prayer and Bible reading.
   - Ask, Historically, which of these indicators are you most likely to encounter?
     - As a follow-up to each reply, ask, Can you tell about a specific time when you allowed that indicator to turn you to the Lord? And if so, what came of it?
10. Ask participants to share what they highlighted or found meaningful in chapter 3.
11. Assign the reading of chapter 4 and close in prayer.

SESSION 4
(A discussion of what was read in chapter 4)

1. Begin on time.
   - Open in prayer, thanking God for Anita's desire to share about how beneficial it is to seek Him daily. Ask Him to give you and each person within the group a fresh determination to do so.
2. Read aloud 1 Peter 3:15 (AMP): "In your hearts, set Christ apart [as holy—acknowledging Him, giving Him first place in your lives] as Lord."
   - Ask, Is this something that comes without effort, or does it require it? Explain.
   - Ask, What evidence suggests you are truly setting your heart on Jesus as Lord, on giving God priority in your life?
   - Ask, Why do you think it's so easy for many professing Christians to bump God to a position of low priority in terms of how they do life?
3. Have all participants turn to p. 78 for their answers to chapter 4's Topical Reflections questions.
   - Ask, Which of Anita's five steps for having a successful quiet time do you think would prove most helpful to you if you adopted it? Explain.
   - Ask for a show of hands revealing who agrees or disagrees with this statement: "The conditions of dawn and communion with God go together."[2]
     - Discuss the pros and cons of starting the day in prayer and Scripture.
4. Encourage everyone to take turns sharing about their own favorite "spots" to meet with God. Be sure to point out that

---

[2] Oswald Chambers, *My Utmost Devotional Bible* (Nashville: Thomas Nelson, 1997), 302 (see chap. 5, n. 5).

having a particular spot is a suggestion—not a rule. God is *omnipresent*, that is, everywhere present.
5. Ask participants to share how many minutes they feel it takes to have a sufficient quiet time with God.
   - Ask, Should we always stop fellowshipping with Him when a timer goes off? Why or why not?
6. Request that a volunteer read Romans 3:22–23 and 3:10.
   - Ask, How might these passages be used in support of the idea that no believer is excluded from Jesus's Great Commission call in Matthew 28:19–20?
7. Ask for volunteers to share about times when something they learned while fellowshipping with God gave them opportunity to speak His truth or made them more confident about sharing the gospel itself.
   - Verbally praise God for the way He prepares us today for what's coming tomorrow.
8. Note that Anita spoke about a time when she shared about Christ and His Word on a plane, though she felt totally inadequate to do so.
   - Ask, What comfort did you find in her story?
   - Ask, How does 2 Corinthians 12:8–10 apply to the topic of feeling inadequate?
9. Point out that chapter 4 incorporated many quotations and some other powerful stories to emphasize our need to prioritize daily time with God. Ask participants to identify which ones spoke the loudest to them and why.
10. Ask participants to share what else they highlighted or found meaningful in chapter 4.
11. Assign the reading of chapter 5 and close in prayer.

SESSION 5
(A discussion of what was read in chapter 5)

1. Begin on time.
   - Open in prayer, thanking God for the amazing honor and generous benefits of belonging to and spending time with Him. Ask Him to help all of you choose to live in such a way as to express gratitude.
2. Encourage participants to consider their closest relationships, whether with spouses, children, parents, or best friends.
   - Ask, What experiences have most contributed to the closeness you enjoy with those people?
   - Point out that just as experiencing camaraderie with others requires investments of time and energy, intimacy with God does too.
   - Ask, What illustration did Anita give to support the idea that we can grow close to someone even without the benefits of seeing them in person?
3. Have everyone turn to chapter 5 and flip through the pages slowly, listing aloud the eight rewards Anita found as a result of investing daily in her relationship with God.
   - Ask, Which reward is most appealing to you? Why?
4. Note aloud that you want to explore several of these points further. Mention that the apostle Paul taught that believers are to have "the mind of Christ" (1 Corinthians 2:16), that we are to choose to let what God has to say on a subject transform the way we think.
   - Share about a time when Christ transformed your own thinking to be more in line with His as you spent time with Him in Bible reading and prayer.
   - Encourage participants to share about specific instances in which Christ transformed their thoughts based on the truth of His Word.

5. Request that a volunteer read aloud Isaiah 26:3. Before she begins, point out that the "you" mentions in the passage are references to God.
   - Ask, With this verse in mind, what might a lack of inner peace in our lives suggest?
   - Ask participants to share about specific times when they've experienced God's peace as they've chosen to trust in His Word as truth.
   - Ask, Why do you think Isaiah 9:6 refers to Jesus as the "Prince of Peace"?
6. Direct participants to pp. 91–92 for reference. Ask, What most stood out to you in Anita's discussion of God's will?
7. Ask, How helpful was it to you to hear that spiritual gifts are not the same as talents?
   - Encourage participants to try to identify their spiritual giftings based on the information on p. 92.
   - Ask, What is the main thing God wants us to do with our spiritual gifts, whatever they may be? *(Direct them to 1 Peter 4:10 if they need help.)*
   - Request that several volunteers share about how they've used their spiritual gifts in the past and how doing so ended up not just benefiting others but also aiding their own spiritual walks.
8. Remind participants that Anita's young son so associated the word *joy* with her that he thought it was her middle name.
   - Ask, What evidence might lead someone to give you the nickname "Joy"?
   - Have a volunteer read Philippians 4:4–8 aloud in support of the idea that joy and peace are to be important components in the Christian's life, even in hard times.
     - Ask, Do you think it's possible for someone to be joyful always? Explain.

- Ask, What practical changes might we make to help us live with more Godward focus and less anxiety?
9. Share about a time when you were blessed because someone else walked closely with Jesus.
    - Encourage participants to share similar stories of their own.
10. Ask participants to share what else they highlighted or found meaningful as they read chapter 5.
11. Assign the reading of chapter 6 and close in prayer.

SESSION 6

(A discussion of what was read in chapter 6)

1. Begin on time.
   - Open in prayer, praising God for the blessing of being His children and asking for His help and grace in dodging and overcoming the enemy's tactics to hinder spiritual growth.
2. Request that a volunteer read aloud the apostle Paul's words in Philippians 3:14.
   - Ask, How does this verse support the idea that the Christian life is like a race down a long path?
   - Ask, Why do you think Satan is so opposed to believers making spiritual progress? Why does he care?
3. Request that participants respond to this statement by writer Thomas C. Peters: "Satan's greatest victories do not lie in getting unbelievers to heap vice upon vice, but in lulling believers into taking God's Word lightly."[3]
   - Ask participants to briefly explain instances of how they've seen Peters's quote prove true in their own lives.
   - Ask, What does the enemy's love of getting us to question the trustworthiness of Scripture suggest about the importance of spending time in God's Word and in prayer, of building our faith muscles?
4. Ask, Are you most likely to (a) get sidetracked by distraction once you sit down to quiet time or (b) get sidetracked by busyness beforehand?
   - Ask, What is it specifically that distracts you from quiet time in one way or another?
     - Encourage participants to suggest practical ways to deal with each thing that's mentioned, but remain on guard against letting the discussion take on a judgmental tone.

---

[3] Thomas C. Peters, *Cherish the Word: Reflections on Luther's Spirituality* (St. Louis: Christian Publishing House, 2000), 62 (see chap. 6, n. 2).

- Ask, What help do Nehemiah 6:3 and Luke 10:38–42 offer us in the fight against busyness and distraction?
5. Have participants turn to pp. 112–113, to the list of possible fears that might keep someone from seeking God faithfully. Point out which one you best identify with and why.
    - Request that volunteers either identify which of the fears are most likely to discourage them or share other fears that do.
6. Encourage participants to take turns looking up and reading these Bible passages about fear that the Lord included in His file for us:
    - Deuteronomy 31:8
    - Isaiah 41:13
    - Psalm 27:1–3
    - Psalm 46:1–3
    - Psalm 118:6–7
    - John 14:27 (Jesus speaking)
        - Ask, Which of these verses most spoke to you?
        - Ask, How might memorizing verses like these help us to cope with fear?
        - Ask, Why would it be a good idea to send one of these passages to a Christian friend struggling with fear or anxiety?
7. Note aloud how Anita equated worldliness with a thorny bramble running alongside one's spiritual path.
    - Ask, What are some specific temptations that can lead Christians—even deeply committed Christians—to run into such thorns?
    - Ask, What should we do when we feel the sting of consequences brought on by personal sins?
    - Ask, What does 1 Peter 2:11 warn us of concerning sinful desires?
        - Ask, How might that image help you in the future?

- Request that a volunteer read Paul's similar warning and advice to believers in Ephesians 6:10–18.
  › Ask, What do you find most helpful in that passage?
8. Launch a discussion of why we must deal with our old fleshly nature sometimes, even after receiving a new nature through having God's Holy Spirit within us. Specifically address what purpose such tension might serve.
    - Ask, What will end this inner battle between flesh and Spirit?
9. Note aloud that theologian Warren Wiersbe said, "Once you have begun to cultivate this deeper communion with Christ, you will have no desire to return to the shallow life of a careless Christian."[4]
    - Ask, In light of the battle between the flesh and Spirit and all the enemy tactics we've been discussing, what hope do you find in Wiersbe's words?
10. Ask participants to share what else they highlighted or found meaningful as they read chapter 6.
11. Assign the reading of chapter 7 and close in prayer.

---

[4] Warren W. Wiersbe, *Bible Exposition Commentary*, vol. 1 (Colorado Springs: David C. Cook, 2003), 355 (see chap. 6, n. 13).

SESSION 7
(A discussion of what was read in chapter 7)

1. Begin on time.
   - Open in prayer, thanking God very specifically for who He is and what He does.
2. Ask, What specific things did Anita's three reminders encourage us to avoid doing with regard to quiet time?
   - What commonality do these share?
3. Request that a volunteer read Malachi 1:6–14 aloud.
   - Ask, What was at the heart of God's frustration with these people?
   - Ask, Can you identify a specific instance since you accepted Christ in which you failed to treat God as the great King He is? If so, explain.
   - Ask, What is the best response to all such personal failures?
     - Ask, What hope does Psalm 103:10–13 offer us believers as we wrestle with our sins?
4. Ask for a volunteer to summarize Anita's story about the young man in the country church meeting.
   - Ask, What lessons did Anita take away from that encounter?
   - Encourage participants to share about times when the childlike faith or limited physical capacity of another believer similarly challenged their hearts.
   - Ask, Do you think God expects us to get everything right, all the time, this side of Heaven?
     - Ask, Why might it prove spiritually and morally motivating to remember that God offers us grace and understands our limitations and our tendencies to fail?
5. Ask, What are the dangers of working through a study like this one or even using a daily devotional *in your quiet time* rather than just reading the Bible itself?

- Encourage participants always to spend the bulk of their Bible study time in the Bible, noting specific ways you've found that helpful.
- Hold up a study Bible. Then flip through it, pointing out to the group that only the biblical text that comprises the bulk of the printing is God's inspired, trustworthy Word, what 2 Timothy 3:16–17 refers to. The articles, maps, and commentary are helpful, yet they are not God's perfect Scripture; they are later additions that do not bear the same weight.
  - Ask, Why is it important to know that?
6. Encourage participants to discuss why God is not to be equated with a genie at our service.
   - Request that a volunteer read James 1:2–4.
     - Ask, What light does this shed on why we shouldn't expect God to deliver us from all trials as a genie-on-call might?
7. Acknowledge aloud the link Anita suggested between Christian leaders falling from grace and her reminder that quiet time is not the time to cram for a Bible lesson. Then share about a time when your own spiritual busyness of some sort stood between you and God.
   - Ask, What can we all do to avoid having things like that happen as we minister?
8. Request that a volunteer read aloud the A. W. Tozer quote on p. 133.
   - Ask, What might we do to keep this from being said of us individually?
9. Note aloud that preacher and writer Oswald Chambers said, "There is only one relationship that matters, and that is your personal relationship to a personal Redeemer and Lord."[5]

---

[5] Oswald Chambers, *My Utmost Devotional Bible* (Nashville: Thomas Nelson, 1997), 361 (see chap. 5, n. 5).

- Ask, Do you believe that's true or not? Explain your reasoning.
  - If participants are divided or find the quote to be untrue, ask, How might prioritizing our relationship with God above everyone and everything else—even our marriages—actually prove beneficial to all our relationships in the long run?
10. Ask participants to share what else they highlighted or found meaningful as they read chapter 7.
11. Assign chapter 8 and close in prayer.

SESSION 8

(A discussion of what was read in chapter 8, along with encouragement for those beginning the 21-Day Challenge)

In preparation for this session, plan a party for your group. The goal is to offer participants a tangible celebration of the exciting decision they are making to seek God daily from this study forward. Use balloons and crepe paper, for instance, to make your meeting area festive. Invite participants to bring finger foods and desserts to class. Assemble "graduation kits" that include quiet-time helps like crayon pencils, individual servings of tea, pocket tissues, fun kitchen timers, and spiral books of lined index cards that can aid memory work.

1. Begin on time.
   - Open in prayer, praising God for the honor of getting to live as a student of His Word and asking His blessing on this final session.
   - Point out that this session has a celebratory theme because you are excited about what each participant will gain as she keeps better anchoring herself in God's Word, as she's now fully prepared to do.
2. Note that Psalm 119:105 says, "[God's] word is a lamp for my feet, a light on my path."
   - Ask, In what specific ways has God's Word illuminated your world or showed you which way to go as you've studied it over these last weeks?
     - Encourage respondents to describe how it feels to have the Bible speak directly to their hearts.
3. Request that a volunteer read Hebrews 4:12–13 aloud.
   - Ask, What does it mean that "the word of God is alive and active" (v. 12)?

- Request that volunteers share about instances when something in God's Word, that they may have read dozens of times previously, suddenly impacted them in a new and meaningful way.
  - Point out that such experiences are evidence that God's Word is as "alive and active" as it claims.
4. Ask, How might it help us to always read the Bible as if it's the first time we've seen it?
   - Ask, How does it help us to recall what we already know of Scripture as we read?
5. Lead a discussion of how the fuller routine Anita introduced in chapter 8 differs from the basic one in chapter 4. See pp. 69 and 152 for a comparison of each.
   - Ask, What aspect of the more-complex chapter 8 model do you think will prove most helpful to you in the long run?
6. Have participants get out the Joy Journals they've been using in quiet time. Request that those who feel confident doing so share their favorite reflections on either Proverbs 31 or something they've already studied in John's Gospel—which is the focus of the 21-Day Challenge.
7. Encourage everyone to share about specific ways they've responded to God for things He's already shown them during quiet times.
   - Ask, What does responding back to the Lord before we move on with our days accomplish?
8. Ask, Was there a change your reading of God's Word urged you to make this week that you feel resistant to? If so, explain.
   - Ask, Generally speaking, what should we do when our wants, ideas, and opinions fail to line up with Scripture?
   - Point out that anytime we think something about the Bible itself is off, the problem is our limited understanding—never God's Word. Encourage humility on this matter, perhaps by sharing about a time when the Lord eventually filled in gaps

Leader's Guide 177

in your understanding to show that the Bible was right all along.
9. Encourage participants to share what else they highlighted or found meaningful as they read chapter 8.
10. Encourage those who've already begun the 21-Day Challenge to stay the course, and urge those who haven't to give it a try.
    - Thank everyone for their faithful attendance and participation over these last weeks.
    - Direct attention to p. 184 for Anita's email address should participants like to share what they're learning with her and the JoyShop team.
11. Close in prayer.

APPENDIX

HOW TO KNOW YOU ARE GOD'S CHILD

FRIEND, I WANT to invite you to have a personal relationship with Jesus Christ, to make the one decision that changes a person from an enemy of God into a beloved heir. If you can't say with confidence that you have God's forgiveness and will one day live with Him in Heaven, I pray you'll take these next simple steps. Placing faith in Jesus and crossing over from death to life really is as easy as ABC.

A. Admit you're a sinner who needs God's help.
In Romans 3:23 the Bible says, "All have sinned and fall short of the glory of God." All the bad things we do, from entertaining thoughts of lust or revenge to mistreating others, is sin. It's sin that separates us from God, our Creator. So own the things you do that are displeasing to Him. Only then are you ready to accept the fact that you need His grace. This puts you in a position to repent, to turn from sin and toward God.

B. Believe that Jesus, God's Son, is the Lord over all things; He died on the cross <u>for you</u> and rose from the grave three days later.
In John 3:16–17 the Bible says, "God so loved the world that he

gave his one and only Son, that whoever believes in him shall not perish but have eternal life. For God did not send his Son into the world to condemn the world, but to save the world through him." Sinless Jesus died on a cross so that sin's dominance over our lives could be defeated; amazingly, He took the punishment we deserved! He rose from the grave to show that all who trust in Him will triumph over death. How? Because the penalty for their sin has been paid! John 1:12 says, "To all who did receive [Jesus], to those who believed in his name, he gave the right to become children of God." And John 20:31 adds "that Jesus is the Messiah, the Son of the God, and that by believing you may have life in his name." There's no other means through which people can get into right relationship with God. There's no other path to Heaven. Jesus is the only way (see John 14:6).

C. Confess Jesus as Lord of your life and commit to following Him.

In Romans 10:9 the Bible says, "If you declare with your mouth, 'Jesus is Lord,' and believe in your heart that God raised him from the dead, you will be saved." That means that by confessing your sins to Him and sincerely choosing to call Jesus your Lord, you really are saved from living under God's wrath toward your sin and are instead given His forgiveness. As if that weren't enough, you will one day be welcomed into Heaven.

In the meantime, you can prove that your acceptance of Him is authentic through obeying His Word and doing the good works He has planned for you (see John 14:23; Ephesians 2:10; and the advice in this book). Obedience and good works do nothing to save us or keep us saved; Jesus declared that work "finished" (John 19:30). Nevertheless, they do express gratitude to God for what He has done for us through Jesus. They also help us point others to Him.

If you read through the above points and feel a stirring in

your heart, please pray to accept Jesus as Lord of your life. Doing so might sound something like this:

> *Heavenly Father, I admit I haven't lived for You as I should. I'm a sinner. And today I confess my sins—those in my thoughts, those that have come out of my mouth, and those actions that displease You. I believe Your Son, Jesus, died on the cross to take the punishment I deserve and rose three days later to show that through believing in Him I can have Your forgiveness and will one day defeat death itself. So today I want to make Jesus my Lord and Savior. Please send Him into my heart and make me clean. I confess that I need Him. And I ask that from this day forward, You'll give me a desire to seek more of You, to live in the way You want me to live, and to tell others about You. Help me to trust and follow Your way, dear God, my Father. I want to live for You. Amen.*

If you prayed that or something similar and sincerely meant it, you're saved from your sin and guaranteed Heaven, and you have been "born again" as a new person free from condemnation (John 3:3; see Romans 8:1). So pause for a moment and rejoice! You may even want to mark this occasion by signing and dating this page. The Bible tells us that the names of those who accept Jesus as Lord are written down in His Book of Life and that there is rejoicing in Heaven every time a person places faith in Him (see Luke 15:10).

Anita Keagy, who received training from Precept Ministries co-founder Kay Arthur as well as from Anne Graham Lotz, started JoyShop Ministries in 2006. She has one passionate mission: to inspire people to spend daily time with God through Bible reading and prayer. Since then, she's traveled the world, sharing her message of how to seek God first each day as the key to experiencing abundant life, joy, and peace. Thousands have heard and responded to her dynamic message at conferences, retreats, school chapel services, and church gatherings.

Today Anita lives in rural Pennsylvania with her husband, Paul, where they are blessedly surrounded by their four adult children—Shelly, Carrie, Josh, and Ryan—their spouses, and many grandchildren. Additionally, her first daughter, Twila, and her extended family live locally as well, a gift from the Lord.

Bethany McShurley is a freelance writer and editor who loves to spread the message that a relationship with Jesus can radically transform every aspect of life. She lives near Nashville with her husband, Jon, and two teenage sons, Aidan and Tristan. Bethany specializes in Bible-based resources and can be reached through her website: faithbasedediting.com.

A Personal Invitation to Partner with JoyShop

Thank you for taking the time to participate in this study that's so dear to my heart! Many people ask how they can support JoyShop Ministries, enabling my team and me to get this message into the hands of new audiences. If you are among that generous group, please consider helping us spread the desire to seek God first through one of the following ways:

- **PRAY** for JoyShop Ministries. We know we can do nothing without God's help.
- **PROCLAIM** what God has done in your life as a result of applying the ideas in this book. Visit our website, joyshop.org, and send me an email at info@joyshop.org so I can hear from and celebrate with you. *Please use "Good Report!" as your subject line*, and let me know whether it's okay to use your recommendation as part of our marketing and outreach efforts.
- **PARTNER** with us financially. You can donate online or purchase related materials at www.joyshop.org.

May God bless you for your support!

Much love,
Anita Keagy and Team